Y0-CAS-539

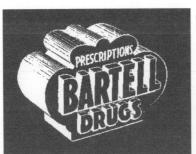

BARTELL DRUGS
BARTELL'S

BARTELL DRUGS

Bartell's
BREAKFAST MENU

Bartell's
TEA ROOM

Bartell's

BARTELL'S

Bartell

BARTELL DRUGS

125 YEARS OF SERVICE

THE BARTELL STORY

FOUNDED BY GEORGE BARTELL

1890~2015

Phil Dougherty & The HistoryLink Staff

The Bartell Story
125 Years of Service

Phil Dougherty & The HistoryLink Staff

© 2014, Bartell Drug Company. All Rights Reserved.

Project manager and editor: Tom Brown
Design: Nancy Kinnear, Marie McCaffrey
Copy editor: Charles Smyth
Index: Michael Billings Townley
Photographic research: Phil Dougherty

A HistoryLink book

Published by Bartell Drug Company in association with Historylnk / HistoryLink.org

HistoryLink.org, the online encyclopedia of Washington State history

Printed and bound in China
First printing: October 2014
ISBN 0-9788302-9-6

The paper used in this publication meets the minimum requirements of American National Standard for Information Sciences—Permanence of Paper for Printed Library Materials, ANSI Z39.48-1984. ∞

CONTENTS

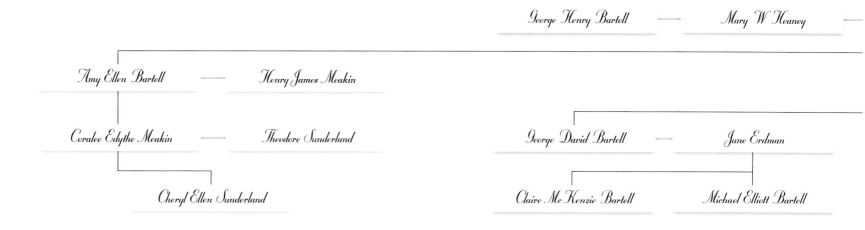

George Henry Bartell — Mary W Heaney

Amy Ellen Bartell — Henry James Meakin

Coralee Edythe Meakin — Theodore Sunderland

George David Bartell — June Erdman

Cheryl Ellen Sunderland

Claire McKenzie Bartell   Michael Elliott Bartell

FOREWORD

Frank A. Blethen

THE BARTELL STORY
125 YEARS OF SERVICE

The Bartell Story is a magnificent case study of one of Puget Sound's most valuable institutions and of the remarkable stewardship of three generations of the Bartell family. Few things are more valuable to a community than locally owned family businesses — especially the rare multigenerational ones.

Never have they been more important to our community than today, as we continue to suffer the ills from decades of unfettered transfer of local economic power to absentee consolidators epitomized by Wall Street — a trend that has eroded our local sense of community, our jobs and our tax base.

Having spent my career in a multigeneration family business and having studied family businesses for thirty-five years, I can attest to the significance of the Bartells' 125-year stewardship. Indeed, only about 15 percent of family businesses endure to the third generation. After that, it's so rare our government doesn't even try to track the survivors.

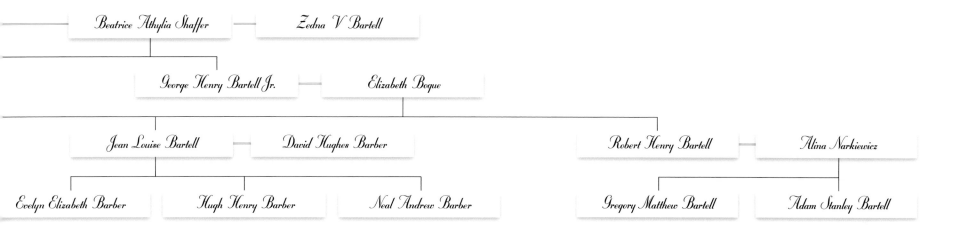

Kudos to George D. Bartell and Jean Bartell Barber for their unusual candor about family dynamics, and the challenges and perils faced by their company across more than twelve decades. Few family business stewards are willing to be this candid. Yet it is essential if the reader is to understand the complexities of a successful multigenerational family business.

A successful family business must constantly adapt — whether it's responding to generational transitions, ever-evolving competition, government regulations, changing customer needs, wars, or economic downturns. All the while, the family stewards must stay true to core principles around community, employees and customers. They must always maintain a long-term view toward service and stewardship rather than the all-too-common impulse to chase short-term financial gain and personal aggrandizement.

From pharma to tearooms to photo processing to flu shots and cholesterol tests, the Bartell family gives us a rare look at successful adaptation.

Ironically, the primary reason family businesses fail or are assimilated by Wall Street is federal and state tax policies that make it impossible for all but a handful of passionate, values-based families to perpetuate their businesses and all the community benefits they provide.

George and Jean are unsung community heroes. Bartell's with its sixty-three locations and seventeen hundred employees is a local treasure. I am putting my money on another successful transition to their family's fourth generation — 125 years of community service and counting.

Frank A. Blethen
Publisher, *The Seattle Times*
Fourth Generation Blethen Family Steward

Looking north on 2nd Avenue from Yesler Way, ca. 1905.
Bartell's Owl Drugstore is visible on the extreme right.

BY PHIL DOUGHERTY

INTRODUCTION

The Bartell story is in many ways part of the Seattle story. George Bartell opened his first drugstore in 1890 on Jackson Street in Seattle, in what is now the city's Leschi neighborhood. As Seattle was small in 1890, so was Bartell's first store. As Seattle grew in leaps and bounds in the ensuing 125 years, so did Bartell Drugs. As Seattle occasionally suffered setbacks and slowdowns, so did Bartell Drugs. As Seattle eventually expanded into Greater Seattle, Bartell Drugs followed. Today, the Bartell Drug Company isn't just a Seattle institution; it's a Puget Sound region institution.

Though George Bartell had only a basic elementary education, he had boundless energy as well as an innate ability to make a personal connection with nearly everyone he met. These talents enabled him to turn his small drugstore into a thriving company with more than twenty stores during his lifetime. His son, George Bartell Jr., was better educated but more reserved than his father. Yet he was astute enough not to try to mimic his father's ways. Instead he brought in the right mix of talent to help pull the company out of a two-decade slump, probably surprising more than a few in the process. His children, George D. Bartell and Jean Bartell Barber, have made their own imprint on Bartell Drugs in a second century that so far has brought steady growth and stability to the company.

The Bartell family is quick to give equal credit to their employees for the company's success, be it the straightforward Val Storrs, who played a major role in helping return the company to prosperity in the 1960s and 1970s, or the always upbeat Gordon O'Reilly, who played an equally big role during these years, or the no-nonsense Sanford Barnes, who managed Bartell's downtown triangle store for nearly twenty years. Many other employees also made substantial contributions, and their discipline and perseverance made a difference.

But Bartell's will always tell you that the customer is the boss, and the company has emphasized its customer service throughout its history. This personal, even-handed touch has resonated with its customers, and they've responded to help make Bartell Drugs one of Seattle's eminent companies. And this distinction comes in a city with many noteworthy companies.

For most of Seattle's history Bartell's has been there, a steady presence that millions have relied on without a second thought. From being the place to go for a plug of opium to numb a sore tooth in the 1890s, to the place to be for a soda or a hot meal during World War II, to the place to get prescriptions and vaccinations in the twenty-first century, Bartell's has always meant something to Seattle.

Today, Bartell Drugs has dozens of pharmacies serving not only Seattle and King County but Pierce and Snohomish counties too. Its 125 years in business have earned Bartell's the distinction of being the oldest family-owned pharmacy chain in the United States.

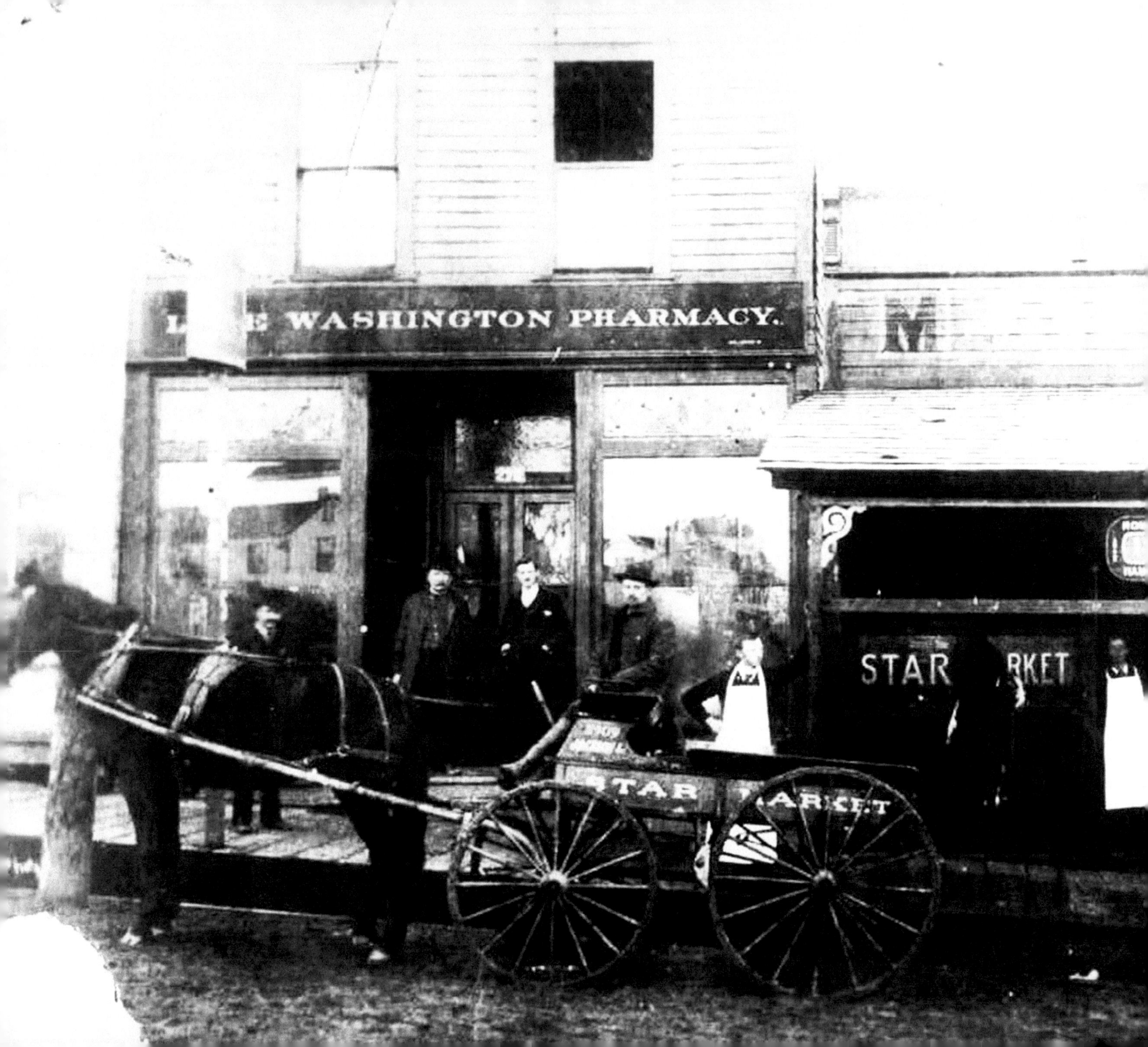
WASHINGTON PHARMACY.
STAR
RKET
STAR
ARKET

CHAPTER 1

Setting Up Shop
(1868–1899)

George Henry Bartell was born on December 14, 1868, in Dickinson County, Kansas, to Augustus and Mary Ann Branscome Bartell. He was the sixth of ten children. Augustus Bartell had immigrated to the United States from Germany with his family in 1832, when he was still a baby. He married Mary Ann Branscome in Iowa in 1856, but by 1860 they were living in Kansas. The Bartells briefly moved to California in the mid-1860s but didn't stay long. They were back in Kansas by the time of George's arrival, settling in Dickinson County, which later became known as the county where President Dwight Eisenhower grew up. In the early 1870s, the family moved one county east to Junction City, Kansas, and established a farm there. By 1880, Augustus Bartell co-owned a hotel in the town and also was dealing in lumber.

Augustus and Mary Ann Bartell had seven girls and three boys. George had an older brother, but he died as a child. This left George as the oldest surviving son. As a result he bore the brunt of many of the farming responsibilities dealt out by his father. But he was not happy in this situation and struck out on his own as soon as he could. At age 14, with only a seventh-grade education, he left. Though startlingly young by today's standards, a 14-year-old male finishing school and setting out on his own was not unusual in 1883. If anything, it was expected. In Junction City in 1883, children completed elementary school after seventh grade, and statistics from the year before show that fewer than 10 percent of the town's students went on to high school. This was hardly unique to Junction City. Most American students didn't go to high school in the nineteenth century, and if they didn't — at least if they were male — they went to work.

OPPOSITE: *The Lake Washington Pharmacy at 2911 Jackson Street in the early 1890s.*

ABOVE: *Augustus Bartell (left), Mary Ann Bartell*

Bartell traveled about seventy miles west to Lincoln County, where he found a job as a drugstore assistant. Yet there was a bit more to it than that. He explained in an interview late in life, "A friend of mine advised me to enter the drug business when I was very young, and I got acquainted with the president at that time of the state pharmaceutical association and he took me under his wing." Bartell's mentor — who happened to own the drugstore in Lincoln — saw the young man's potential and trained him well. After two years he was promoted to assistant manager of the drugstore. At 18 he became a licensed pharmacist after completing a year's apprenticeship.

ABOVE, TOP: *Corner 2nd Avenue and Cherry Street looking south in June 1889, shortly after the Great Seattle Fire. Note all of the temporary tents in the pictures that were set up for businesses to continue operating.*

ABOVE: *A locomotive near the new Stampede Pass Tunnel, ca. 1888.*

OPPOSITE: *Seattle's first streetcar, September 1884.*

ABOVE: *A family sketch of George Bartell as a teenager in the 1880s.*

Seattle in the 1880s

In 1880, Seattle was still a small town — its population a mere 3,533. It wasn't even the largest town in Washington Territory (that honor went to Walla Walla, which had a whopping fifty-five more people). But during the 1880s, and especially in the final years of the decade, the future Emerald City came into its own.

In 1881, a privately owned water system opened in the city. It was Seattle's first integrated water distribution system, and it operated through the decade. However, it proved woefully inadequate in the city's 1889 fire, leading to the establishment the next year of Seattle's public water system.

The *Madras*, the first steamship to cross the Pacific Ocean from Seattle, departed for Hong Kong in December 1882. The ship returned with hundreds of Chinese laborers aboard, one of several to bring such human cargoes that year. The Chinese were not welcomed. In 1886, a mob of workers attacked these laborers and drove many of them out of Seattle.

In 1885, permanent train service was established between Seattle and Tacoma. More significant, though, was the opening of the Stampede Pass Tunnel in the Cascade Mountains in May 1888, since it provided an improved rail route from Puget Sound to the East. Meanwhile, in Seattle itself, the city's first streetcars — each hauled by a pair of horses — began plodding along 2nd Avenue in 1884. Several other trolley lines followed during the 1880s, including Seattle's first cable-car line in 1887. In 1889, electric cars replaced the horse-drawn streetcars.

Lee Shipyard, the first business on Sand Point, opened about 1886; a number of ships that sailed both Lake Washington and Puget Sound were built there. And regular ferry service began running between Seattle and West Seattle late in 1888, further accelerating the city's development.

In 1887, the total population in King County was about sixteen thousand. But that year, the Northern Pacific Railroad moved its western terminus from Tacoma to Seattle. It was a clear signal that Seattle was the place to be in the Pacific Northwest, and thousands of settlers stampeded into Western Washington. During a two-year period between mid-1887 and mid-1889, King County averaged about nine hundred new arrivals a month. Its population doubled in a year and a half. By sheer coincidence, George Bartell arrived in Seattle just as this influx was beginning.

On June 6, 1889, Seattle's Great Fire wiped out nearly half of downtown Seattle and almost the entire business district. Yet far from dooming the little city, the fire instead provided even more incentives for people to move there. And move they did — between June 1889 and June 1890, Seattle's population leapt from 26,740 to 42,837. New and improved brick buildings were built; sawmills were built and hundreds of new homes followed; roads were cleared and graded, and more trolley lines were added. It was the perfect time for George Bartell to open his Lake Washington Pharmacy.

OPPORTUNITY KNOCKS

Like many Americans in the late nineteenth century, Bartell was lured by the call of the West. In the summer of 1887, he was offered a free ride to Washington Territory in a railroad boxcar in exchange for agreeing to feed ten horses traveling in other boxcars on the train. This opportunity was irresistible for Bartell. He was an energetic, exuberant man who, throughout his life, thrived on taking risks. That's not to suggest he was reckless — far from it. Rather, he was not one to hesitate to make something he wanted happen, and this was it.

Numerous stops stretched out the trip, which ended nearly a month later in Ellensburg, more than a hundred miles east of Seattle. Bartell finished his journey by horseback over Snoqualmie Pass, and arrived in Seattle with $15 in his pocket. He was 18 years old.

His timing couldn't have been better. Seattle in the summer of 1887 was entering both an economic and a population boom that offered all kinds of opportunities to the new arrival. He worked a series of odd jobs, occasionally filled in as a pharmacist, and before long joined forces with a local carpenter, William Carmode, to sell real estate in Seattle, Mercer Island, and Port Blakely. He also managed the books for two local realtors, C. C. Caulkins and George Moore. Gradually Bartell made contacts in his new home and became acclimated to Seattle.

Shortly before the Great Seattle Fire of June 1889, he moved to Whidbey Island to recover from a bout of typhoid fever, which he believed he had contracted from Seattle's water system. Seattle's big fire, though certainly disastrous at the time, actually created a wealth of opportunity in the city. New brick buildings went up, sawmills and brickyards were expanded (and new ones begun), and residential plats were developed. Thousands of job seekers and their families flocked to the city looking for work. Seattle became known as "The Boomingest Place On Earth." Bartell saw the opportunity and returned to the city early in 1890.

THE LAKE WASHINGTON PHARMACY

In late March 1890 Bartell began working part time at the Lake Washington Pharmacy, located at 2911 Jackson Street (later renumbered 2711 S Jackson Street) in what was then considered Seattle's suburbs. Business was better than it otherwise might have been, though, because Seattle's first cable car line (not to be confused with the city's electric trolley lines) ran right by the drugstore. In June, he was hired full time.

The pharmacy owner, Horace Hall, was also a physician. It was common in the nineteenth century for a druggist to be a doctor. This was partly because medical education developed earlier in this country than did pharmacy education, but it also was a reflection of the times. In a far more rural and isolated America than we know today, a pharmacist-physician could prescribe drugs and treat patients on the spot if necessary. But Seattle was big enough and developed enough by 1890 that a doctor could work independently if he wished, and Hall decided to do that. He offered to sell the store to Bartell, who didn't hesitate. A mere two weeks after starting full time at the store, Bartell bought the Lake Washington Pharmacy for $3,000, most of it borrowed. He was 21 years old.

Drugstores in the 1890s were considerably more primitive than they are today or even than what they would be just a few decades later. Bartell hung red and green globes in his storefront windows to identify it as a pharmacy, a common practice of drugstores in the late nineteenth century. In the store's earliest years, he traveled to San Francisco to buy many of his supplies.

In his fifteen-by-thirty-foot store, Bartell sold crude drugs extracted from plants, such as belladonna (used for headaches and cramps) and bloodroot (good for sore throats). He sold catnip, which was brewed into a tea and used to treat colds and fever. He sold bark from cascara trees, which could be used as a laxative, as well as bark from cinchona trees, which was used to treat malaria. Bartell sold oils and medicinal chemicals such as blue mass (which contained mercury), calomel, and ipecac. He sold witch hazel, an astringent often used to reduce inflammation. He also sold saltpeter, which made a handy food preservative in the days before refrigeration.

His store carried a stock of herbs and spices (drugstores typically sold these products in the late nineteenth century, and Bartell Drugs continues to sell a line of inexpensive spices today), and in an era before the automobile, the

ABOVE: *George Bartell, 1890.*

RIGHT: *George Bartell's first listing as a druggist in the Seattle Polk City Directory, 1890.*

OPPOSITE: *Emmet Case (left) and Edward Lawler (right) in front of the Lake Washington Pharmacy, August 1897. Lawler worked for George Bartell between 1895 and 1897, and decades later sent this picture to George Bartell Jr. with a note that "I thought it might be of interest to you."*

Druggists—Retail.
Allen G C, 803 3d.
Ballard Pharmacy, Ballard.
Barnes & Co, 2401 Front.
Bartell G H, 2911 Jackson.
Bentley W R, 1424 Front.
Bolink Elbertus, 319 S 3d.
Brown & Mann, 301 Pike.

store sold horse medicines. Bartell also sold opium (which was legal at the time) to alleviate toothaches. A slice of opium was normally cut for the customer like a plug of tobacco from a fifteen- or twenty-pound slab that Bartell kept in stock.

And he sold patent medicines, "guaranteed" (by the maker, not Bartell) to cure almost any ill. One such well-known medicine was Lydia Pinkham's Vegetable Compound, marketed to women for "ladies' problems" and containing 19 percent alcohol. Another early favorite was Castoria, a laxative for children. Later in the 1890s he sold Peruna, another popular medicine that was used for "catarrh" (congestion of the nose, throat, or lungs); no doubt the medicine's 27 percent alcohol content helped clear those clogged air passages right up.

The store sold candy (two kinds shipped in from New York City), and it sold perfume. It sold a few other cosmetics, such as rose water and face powder, but in the 1890s cosmetics were not

Washington's First Pharmacies

As settlers moved into Washington Territory in the early 1850s, pharmacies followed. But one of the first drug stores in the territory could hardly be classified as a "pharmacy." The owner, Dan Kiser, sold meat on the other side of his store and could easily switch back and forth between the dual role of pharmacist and butcher. Kiser opened his store in 1852 or 1853 in Olympia, but it was soon followed in 1853 by Olympia's first bona fide drugstore, owned by Dr. G. K. Willard. His son, Dr. Rufus Willard, later joined him in the business, and, after his father's death, continued operating it until 1870.

A drugstore also opened in Port Townsend about the same time as in Olympia, stirring some debate over which was first. Port Townsend's store was operated by Dr. Samuel McCurdy, who went on to found the Port Townsend Marine Hospital in 1855. McCurdy also served as surgeon in the Northern Battalion of Washington during the territory's Indian Wars in the mid-1850s.

Seattle's first drugstore, known simply as Kellogg Brothers, was established in 1863 by two brothers, Gardner and David Kellogg. David soon got out of the business, leaving his brother as sole owner. In 1865, Gardner Kellogg opened a new drugstore (initially retaining the name Kellogg Brothers) on the south side of Yesler Way between Occidental Avenue S and 1st Avenue S.

Kellogg worked as a druggist into the 1890s, operating his store under the name Kellogg's Drug Store for many of those years. However, he's actually remembered more for his work as a firefighter. He served as foreman in Seattle's first volunteer fire brigade in 1870, and when the city's fire department was created in 1889, became Seattle's first fire chief.

Another early Seattle pharmacy was the Pioneer Drug Store, opened by Matthew Kelly in about 1870. Kelly is said to have first worked for Dr. Rufus Willard at his drugstore in Olympia, and one source adds that he also worked at Gardner Kellogg's drugstore before opening his own store. The Pioneer Drug Store was on the north side of Yesler Way at the head of 1st Avenue S, across the street and a bit east of the Kellogg drugstore.

Drugs and retail products available in the territory's early pharmacies were far more limited than they are today, and what was available depended in part on where the store was located. Stores in the cities and larger towns could offer more than rural stores, but even these goods were limited.

typically sold in drugstores in the quantities they later would be. In the early years, this suited Bartell just fine. As he explained in a 1950 interview with Seattle's KIRO radio, "I really believed in the ethical drug business and didn't carry much but medicines." However, his inventory changed in the early twentieth century when a surge in available retail products sold at pharmacies and other stores likewise forced Bartell to add them to stay competitive. "The customers are to blame for that for a large measure,"

RIGHT: *Peruna ad, ca. 1900*

LEFT: *The Kellogg and Brother drugstore on Yesler Way shortly after its 1865 opening.*
CENTER: *Gardner Kellogg, an early druggist in Seattle, about the time he became Seattle's first fire chief in 1889.*
BELOW: *A view inside a nineteenth-century drugstore.*

The interior of these early drugstores was usually a long rectangle, with display counters along the perimeter and shelves on the walls. In a few stores these shelves stretched up nearly to the ceiling, requiring clerks to shinny up ladders to reach products there. The store interiors were not as uniform as we know them to be today, though in many cases they still were similar to one another.

Bartell joked with the interviewer. "When people couldn't buy what they wanted [elsewhere]... they'd ask the drugstore if they had it. And by and by we did have it."

In the 1890s, prescription capsules were not yet in common use. This created challenges as to how medicine should be dispensed. Bartell handmade various medications into powders, and he made pills with a pill roller. He folded some of the more unpleasant-tasting medicines in onion skins to try to hide the taste. He also made fluid extracts, tinctures (a plant extract made by soaking herbs in liquid; alcohol was often used because it was a preservative), and mustard plasters.

When capsules came into wider use in the early twentieth century, Bartell initially had to warn his customers not to open them before taking them. The year before he died, he gave an interview to a *Seattle Times* reporter and with a laugh told a story to illustrate his point. "One of my customers complained bitterly about the prescription we'd filled for him. 'Dang it, George,' the fellow said. 'I don't want any more of those capsules; it's way too much work to dig all that powder out of them.' He almost fell over when I told him he should have taken the medicine, capsule and all."

HARD WORK AND A LESSON IN FINANCE

Bartell worked long hours, sometimes twelve to fifteen hours a day, seven days a week, and initially lived in the back of his store building. Yet despite the hard work and long days, he later said he had a lot of fun during this period. The consummate people person who believed the customer was always right, Bartell enjoyed waiting on his customers, who on occasion dropped by his store just to chat. But he found time for other activities. He studied pharmacy at the University of Washington during the first half of the 1890s, when the college was still located in downtown Seattle, but did not earn a degree.

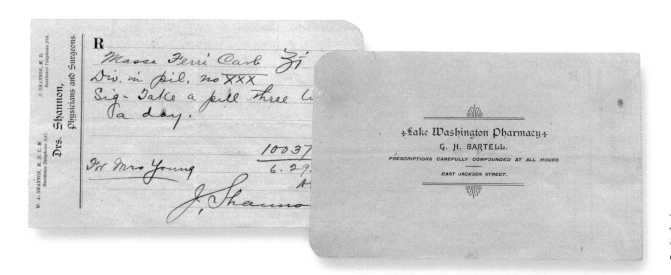

A completed prescription blank from June 1890 by Dr. James Shannon; the Lake Washington Pharmacy is advertised on the back.

At some point during these early years, Augustus Bartell came to Seattle for a visit, and asked his son how the store was doing financially. Young Bartell owned up that he had not worked on his books in a while and couldn't say precisely, although he was still carrying a significant debt load. Indeed he was: When he tallied it up, he found he owed $2,800 to his creditors — only $200 less than what he'd paid to buy the store. Worse, this money was not tied up in store inventory. He really couldn't fully account for it. Augustus Bartell lectured his son on the importance of keeping current on his finances and avoiding debt, a lesson that Bartell later suggested led to the company's policy over the years of conservative financial management. Decades later, this policy would help the company get through the most trying time in its history.

On June 27, 1892, Bartell married Mary Heaney, the first of his three wives, in Seattle. The 1900 U.S. Census records George and Mary Bartell living in a rented house at 1117 31st Avenue S in Seattle, not far from his Lake Washington Pharmacy. Mary Heaney Bartell is something of a mystery. She was born in 1869 in England to Irish parents, and immigrated to the United States in 1870. But little else is known about her or of her marriage to Bartell, other than that they had no children. The marriage ended in the first years of the 1900s, but how it ended (by her death or by divorce) also isn't known.

The Panic of 1893 sent the American economy into a severe four-year depression that would not be rivaled by any other economic downturn in this country until the worldwide Great Depression of the 1930s. But despite the depression, Bartell and his Lake Washington Pharmacy prospered. His hard work and long hours almost certainly helped make the difference, but by 1897, the nonstop working was beginning to affect his health. He hired an assistant, A. E. Casey, that year, but accounts differ whether he hired Casey to help him with his workload or to run the store while he embarked on his next adventure — traveling to the Yukon to join the Klondike Gold Rush.

FROM PHARMACIST TO PROSPECTOR

On July 17, 1897, the steamship *Portland* arrived in Seattle with news of a gold strike in the Canadian Yukon and a ton of gold to prove it. Bartell went down to the ship to see it for himself. Once he did, he (and thousands of others) decided to embark on the Klondike Gold Rush. It was an adventure that he relished for the rest of his life. He quickly gathered the fifteen hundred pounds of supplies that he needed to last for most of the next year. With an additional $2,000 in cash, he boarded the steamer *Queen* for Skagway, Alaska, on July 23, six days after the *Portland* had arrived in Seattle with its golden news.

Arriving in Skagway, Bartell backpacked his supplies over the arduously steep Chilkoot Pass, crossed into Canada, and followed the trail down to Lake Bennett. On the banks of the lake he paired up with a fellow traveler, chopped down trees for a raft, and floated down the Yukon River to Dawson, Yukon Territory. He staked out a claim near Dawson on a tributary of the Yukon River. He and several others then built a small one-room cabin for the winter. The cabin had no floor and a makeshift door that did little to keep out the cold. In fact, one story from Bartell Drugs says that the door fit so poorly that a dog living with the prospectors in the cabin simply crawled under it whenever it wanted in or out.

It was a long winter, with the sun up between four and five hours a day during the shortest days. One day, with an outside temperature approaching 60 below zero, Bartell went to the river to get some water. Though the river was frozen solid, he somehow broke through a weak point in the ice. He managed to scramble out and made it to his cabin, by which time his clothes were frozen solid.

He worked odd jobs in the mines to bring in some cash, and in the spring he was able to work his claim. Although his claim was close to some of the big gold strikes, Bartell did not strike it rich. But he did find enough gold to cover most of the steep expenses of his yearlong trip, and his health improved as a result of all his hard physical work during his trip to the Yukon.

In an interesting aside, the Spanish-American War was fought and won while Bartell was in the Far North. In his later years he enjoyed telling the story of paying 50 cents to listen to a priest read a *Seattle Post-Intelligencer* article about the American naval victory over the Spanish in the Battle of Manila Bay in the Philippines while he was visiting Dawson in the spring or summer of 1898. "It was very interesting to hear," explained Bartell in his homespun style during the 1950 KIRO interview. "He was a good reader."

THE OWL DRUGSTORE

In that same interview, Bartell explained what led him to expand his business when he returned from the Yukon later in 1898. "When I was up in Alaska [sic], I had lots of time to think, and I thought, well, why should I work all the time in the suburbs? Why didn't I go down[town] where there's more business? So immediately when I came back I started a store downtown."

Bartell arrived back in Seattle in the late summer or autumn of 1898 and soon opened his new store at 506 2nd Avenue, just north of Yesler Way. He called his new drugstore "the Owl Drugstore" because a live-in pharmacist was available at all hours of the night to fill a prescription. It was an opportune time for Bartell to make his move. By the end of the 1890s, the American economy was rapidly recovering from the mid-decade depression. Seattle was booming again, and Bartell was perfectly situated to take advantage of it in the heart of the city's downtown. When 1900 arrived, he was doubtlessly looking forward to the new century with a wealth of ideas and the renewed energy to make them happen.

ABOVE: *A view of the southeast corner of 2nd Avenue and James Street shortly after George Bartell opened his Owl Drugstore down the block in 1898. The store is just visible on the right.*

LEFT: *A Bartell Drugs quinine capsule box from the early 1900s. Note the emphasis on service, even in those early days.*

CHAPTER 2

Moving Up
(1900–1919)

In his first big move of the twentieth century, Bartell sold his Lake Washington Pharmacy to 18-year-old Melvin "Bert" Weed in 1900. Weed had worked in the store as a clerk for two years, and had impressed Bartell with his drive and intelligence. The sale proved to be an early example of Bartell's ability to identify promising talent, because Weed ran the store for more than half a century. He moved it a block to 2601 Jackson Street in 1905, named it Weed's Pharmacy in 1910, and operated it until he retired in 1958.

Bartell, meanwhile, had his hands full downtown. Growing his business meant making changes that he hadn't foreseen. By 1902, he was selling some liquor in his drugstore, such as Iler's Malt Whiskey. But it was the dawn of the food-services era that really caught him by surprise, and it was with some trepidation that he opened a soda fountain at the Owl Drugstore that spring. (Ice cream sodas sold for a nickel a glass.) Indeed, in a 1951 interview with *The Seattle Times*, Bartell described it as his most daring venture in adding new lines and services.

"Drugstores didn't serve food in those days in Seattle," he explained. "We heard about some eastern drugstores starting it and some of the boys were anxious to try it. I was a little uneasy but told them to go ahead and they put the thing together. I came down one morning and they were frying eggs. It just about floored me. Now our food business accounts for about a fourth of our business."

Bartell also began expanding product lines. Though the store continued to focus on selling medication, a glance through some of the Bartell ads run during 1902 in *The Seattle Times* shows the nascent trend toward adding nonpharmaceutical products. It was a trend that would transform Bartell's business by the end of the 1920s. By 1902, Bartell was selling sarsaparilla by the bottle,

OPPOSITE: *Bartell's Owl Drugstore on left, ca. 1907.*

ABOVE RIGHT: *Forest's Juniper Tar Compound, a patent medicine sold by Bartell Drugs in the early 1900s for nasal congestion and throat irritation. Its 22 percent alcohol content also made it useful as a disinfectant for small cuts and burns.*

Bay Rum aftershave, Carter's Swedish Hair Renewer, and Crème Loraine, described as a "harmless bleach" for the skin.

BATTLING THE DRUG TRUST

In the early 1900s, Bartell found himself locked in a struggle with what he called the "Seattle Drug Trust," a conglomeration of some forty to fifty drugstores that was a local branch of the National Association of Retail Druggists. The trust set minimum prices for medicine and other products sold in local drugstores and then raised these prices as circumstances permitted, maximizing profits at the expense of the consumer. Bartell bucked the trust and sold his products at his own price.

This put him in the trust's crosshairs. The trust notified wholesale companies on the West Coast that if it discovered them selling to Bartell Drugs, trust members would no longer buy from those wholesalers. A number of wholesalers went along and refused to sell to Bartell, but he was not deterred. He found wholesalers in San Francisco and on the East Coast who would sell to him, and had little trouble keeping his store stocked while he fought the trust.

The battle turned out to be golden for Bartell. A shrewd marketer, he not only fought the trust but made sure the public knew all about it. Between 1901 and 1904, he ran more than a hundred ads in *The Seattle Times* describing his battle with the trust and listing his bargains of the day. He also took the liberty in a few ads of pointing out the trust's price for various items (Carter's Swedish Hair Renewer among them) and then contrasting his lower price.

But the ads were more about the battle, a tale of the little guy standing up to the big bullying behemoth. Some of them were dramatic. "It's some forty against one… Detectives are employed by the Seattle Drug Trust to see who keeps us supplied," reported an ad on January 2, 1902. An ad later that month asserted: "The trusts declared to be grave evils." Others had a patriotic appeal: "[The trusts are] against the teachings of American liberty," argued a February 6 ad, while

another the following month added that trusts "are cowardly and un-American."

And they were all out to get Bartell Drugs. The ads said that the trusts sent detectives on fruitless missions to Portland, Tacoma, and Everett to discover his sources of supplies. The ads also claimed that the trusts encouraged local doctors to discourage their patients from patronizing Bartell Drugs and suggested that the doctors received a commission on their prescriptions that were filled by trust members.

By the spring of 1902, the ads were taking a more humorous bent. "Every time the Bartell Drug Co. receives a carload of medicines the trust druggists become nervously excited," claimed an ad on April 26, while another four days later announced, "A train that

A Train That Brought Tears

The train that brought the carload of medicines to the Bartell Drug Co. yesterday from the East caused agony among the Trust Druggists.

The Poor Fellows

realize that they can't bluff the Eastern Wholesalers as they did the Western Wholesalers into not selling to us.

A Few Anti-Trust Prices

Paine's Liver Pills, 25c size 10c
S. S. S., $1.00 size 58c
Peruna, $1.00 size 58c
Red Cross Skin Soap, 35c size 20c
Ice Cream Soda, per glass 5c

Boycotted by the Seattle Drug Trust, composed of fifty stores

Free Delivery.   Phone Main 503.
506 SECOND AVE.

LEFT: *A Bartell antitrust ad in* The Seattle Times *in 1902 kept the "trust druggists" in an unwelcome spotlight.*

OPPOSITE, LEFT: *An undated photo of the Bartell family home at 1517 11th Avenue W in Seattle.*

RIGHT: *Beatrice Shaffer as a young woman, ca. 1900.*

brought tears — the train that brought the carload of medicines to the Bartell Drug Co. yesterday from the East caused agony among the Trust Druggists."

One of the ads summarizes George Bartell's personality and his philosophy: "Men who wait for someone to tell them how to run their affairs belong to a class of unsuccessfuls," read a June 2, 1902, ad. It was a philosophy that Bartell followed until his final days. As *The Seattle Times* explained in its 1951 article, "He looks ahead, never over his shoulder."

A couple of other local drugstores — the Quaker Drug Company and Seattle druggist G.O. Guy — later ran a few similar ads in *The Seattle Times*; the Quaker ads bore a remarkable resemblance to the Bartell ads. Still, Bartell's ads were quintessentially his, and they worked, attracting hundreds of new customers to Bartell Drugs. By 1904, the trust was starting to lose its clout, and by the end of 1907, it was defunct. Bartell later remarked, "After that, we just seemed to grow with Seattle."

Patent medicine manufacturers also were affected by the demise of the trust, as they too had had a hand in trying to regulate the prices of their proprietary medicines. At the same time, rising public outcry for federal regulation of the drug industry led to the passage of the Pure Food and Drug Act in 1906, which directly impacted the patent medicine industry. Though the act did not prohibit the sale of patent medicines, their ingredients now had to be disclosed and false advertising was prohibited. As a result, public attitudes toward patent medicines changed, and their popularity began to decline.

GEORGE BARTELL MARRIES BEATRICE SHAFFER

On October 18, 1905, Bartell married Beatrice Shaffer. She was a native of Helena, Montana, and the daughter of Fisk Shaffer, a noted Helena architect and contractor who designed and built homes and buildings in Helena during the final three decades of the

THE DRUG TRUST

What was this nefarious Seattle Drug Trust that George Bartell battled in the early twentieth century? It was just a nickname that he used to refer to the Seattle Retail Druggists Association, a local branch of the National Association of Retail Druggists. NARD was founded in 1898 to stop the expansion of aggressive price-discounting by druggists and to promote the concept of "fair trade," which, in essence, tried to set minimum prices for various pharmaceutical items.

The Seattle Retail Druggists Association was formed not long after NARD, and by 1901, some forty drugstores had joined. This association was said to have used a variety of heavy-handed tactics against those who bucked it. Its efforts failed, however, because the association was neither big enough nor strong enough to corner the market.

But the reality is that the drug trust represented not just one local association but a number of them, including many on the national level. Perhaps the three biggest players in the trust were NARD, the National Wholesale Druggists Association, and the Proprietary Association of America. In 1906, the Department of Justice sued the trust and eventually brought ninety-seven defendants into the litigation. The

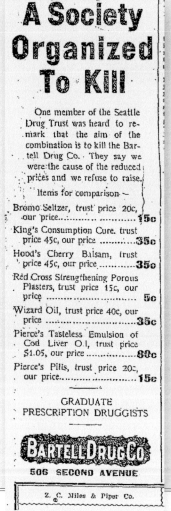

A Society Organized To Kill

One member of the Seattle Drug Trust was heard to remark that the aim of the combination is to kill the Bartell Drug Co. They say we were the cause of the reduced prices and we refuse to raise.

Items for comparison —

Bromo-Seltzer, trust price 20c, our price..................**15c**

King's Consumption Cure, trust price 45c, our price............**35c**

Hood's Cherry Balsam, trust price 45c, our price...........**35c**

Red Cross Strengthening Porous Plasters, trust price 15c, our price **5c**

Wizard Oil, trust price 40c, our price **35c**

Pierce's Tasteless Emulsion of Cod Liver Oil, trust price $1.05, our price................**80c**

Pierce's Pills, trust price 20c, our price..........................**15c**

GRADUATE PRESCRIPTION DRUGGISTS

BARTELL DRUG CO

506 SECOND AVENUE

Z. C. Miles & Piper Co.

next year, a federal court issued an injunction prohibiting the trust from price-fixing, attempting to restrain the sale of drugs, and blacklisting druggists who cut prices.

NARD next sought legislative support for its effort to maintain higher prices. This was more successful, and in the 1930s and 1940s, state and federal laws were passed that required a pharmacist to sell products subject to the law at or above a minimum price set by the manufacturer. These laws met with mixed success. Many druggists simply ignored them, and by 1975, they had all been repealed.

The Seattle Retail Druggists Association survived until at least 1940. And NARD still exists today, although it is now known as the National Community Pharmacists Association, or NCPA. The NCPA is a far broader association than it was in its original incarnation as NARD. It represents more than twenty-three thousand independent community pharmacies across the United States on a variety of matters, from health-care reform to professional practice issues. Bartell Drugs is currently a member of NCPA.

A Bartell antitrust ad in The Seattle Times, *December 3, 1901.*

nineteenth century. Beatrice was in some respects the opposite of her new husband. A high school graduate, she was an accomplished vocalist and a talented pianist, and had received additional musical training at a Chicago music conservatory. Prior to marrying Bartell she had sung at Seattle social events such as receptions and club teas, at least once as a soprano solo.

The newlyweds moved into a house at 1517 11th Avenue W in Seattle, on the western flank of Queen Anne Hill. The house — still there more than a century later — had been built earlier in the year by Fisk Shaffer. It was large enough to also accommodate

Shaffer and his wife, who lived with the Bartells in the early years of their marriage, an arrangement that didn't work out. Two strong personalities, Fisk Shaffer and George Bartell were unable to get along with each other. Shaffer eventually built a three-story apartment building just south of the house and moved there with his wife.

George and Beatrice Bartell had two children: Amy, born November 30, 1906, and George Jr. — known by his middle name, Henry, as a boy — born nearly ten years later, on October 20, 1916. The Bartell family attempted to get on with their lives, but

the antagonism between Bartell and his father-in-law persisted. George Bartell Jr., in an undated autobiography written around the year 2000, speculated that it was "probably an underlying cause of breakup of my parents' marriage." The Shaffers eventually moved to a farm south of Alderwood Manor, but the Bartells' marriage did not survive, ending in divorce about 1920.

The divorce was amicable. One suspects that in addition to whatever problems the couple had with Fisk Shaffer, Bartell's devotion to his business contributed to the breakup. Yet the two seem to have had little in common. Beatrice was not a conventional early-twentieth century housewife. She was not a cook. She had her own social life. She was much more interested in the arts than Bartell was. She thought nothing of taking her children on hiking trips and picnics up to the Cascades in the 1920s, on rugged roads that were an adventure to drive. And she was shrewd enough to maintain an interest in the Bartell company after the divorce, serving in various officer positions, including president. (Admittedly, this was on paper only. George Bartell was the unquestioned leader of Bartell Drugs until shortly before his death in 1956.)

FOUR THOUSAND BOXES OF CANDY

The Bartell Drug Company formally incorporated on January 23, 1904, and on October 1 of that year, Bartell opened another store.

ABOVE: *Amy and George Bartell Jr. in 1917.*

RIGHT: *A Bartell ad in* The Seattle Times *on September 30, 1904, announced the opening of the Red Cross Annex store.*

This newest store, located at 610 2nd Avenue just north of the Owl Drugstore, was named the Red Cross Annex (and known informally as the main store). It served as Bartell headquarters until 1914. Bartell's Owl Drugstore remained open until 1911, when the building was razed to make way for the Smith Tower.

With the opening of the Red Cross Annex, Bartell again showed his marketing talent. He ran an ad in *The Seattle Times* the evening before, announcing the opening, and added a sweetener: Every customer who made a purchase on opening day, no matter how small, would receive a free box of candy. Bartell bought four thousand boxes to make sure there was plenty, but assured his readers that if he ran out, they would get a voucher they could redeem the following week. The candy hook worked, and Bartell used it frequently over the years as an effective marketing tool when he had a holiday sale or special sale, or opened a new store.

In 1908, Bartell opened a new store on the southwest corner of 1st Avenue and Pike Street, at the entrance to the new Pike Place Market. It was an excellent location, and the store was an important one to the company for many years. It was there for nearly fifty-three years before closing in 1961.

A Decade of Expansion and Change

In May 1910, Bartell opened his first store in Ballard. If he had considered his Lake Washington Pharmacy to be in the suburbs, then he must have considered the Ballard store to be in the hinterlands. Ballard had been an incorporated town until it was annexed by the City of Seattle in 1907, just three years earlier. But his gamble paid off. Bartell's has operated continuously in Ballard since 1910, in four different locations, all within a quarter-mile of one another.

In December 1910, Bartell opened another drugstore at 1416 2nd Avenue. This had been the location of the Raven Drugstore, and it was purchased with Bartell Drug Company stock. The stock purchase created a group of shareholders with a minority interest in the company. Decades later, these minority shareholders and their descendants would cause big problems for Bartell Drugs.

The new store boasted the first Bartell soda fountain to regularly serve hot meals (the Owl Drugstore's soda fountain may have served a hot meal or two, but it was geared more toward ice cream and cold drinks). It was a harbinger of Bartell's food operations, which soon became an integral part of his business. The store also had the dubious distinction of being struck by fire twice in two years. The first fire, in 1911, caused relatively minor damage. In 1912, the store moved down the block into the Denny Building, where it was struck by a more serious fire the following year. Bartell lost $75,000 in inventory in that fire, but he must have been insured, because even with a loss of this magnitude, he was quickly back on his feet.

By this time, Bartell had adopted the practice of numbering his stores and displayed the number of each on the store sign. For example, his store sign on the corner of 1st Avenue and Pike Street read Drug Store No. 3, while a drugstore that he opened in

OPPOSITE, TOP: *A view of Pike Place Market, ca. 1912. The sign for Bartell's Store No. 3 is just visible on the left.*

BELOW: *Bartell cough syrup bottle, ca.1910.*

LEFT: *Looking north on 2nd Avenue from James Street, ca. 1908. Bartell's Red Cross Annex store is in the lower right.*

1921 at 1st Avenue and Yesler Way was Bartell Drugs No. 8. Bartell Drugs continues the numbering tradition today, though the numbers are no longer displayed on the signs.

In 1912, Bartell opened a store on the northwest corner of Westlake Avenue and Pine Street. The Westlake and Pine location proved over the years to be a prime spot for Bartell Drugs. Aside from an eight-year interval between 1922 and 1930, the company had a store in this block (albeit in slightly different locations) until 1984. Its final store there, known as the triangle store because of its distinctive shape, was Bartell's flagship store from its opening in 1935 until 1984, when it was closed and the building was demolished to make way for Westlake Park.

A LIGHTER SIDE

As busy as he was, Bartell found time for fun and leisure. He enjoyed fly fishing and took up golf, probably more for its social aspect than for his actual golfing ability. He later gave it up, commenting, "I was always all over the course except on the fairway." He also was an avid walker, often walking after dinner from his house on Queen Anne Hill to his Ballard drugstore and back, a five-mile round trip.

Bartell was an early member of the Fraternal Order of Eagles, founded in Seattle in 1898. (Many of this organization's earliest members were connected with the theater, a rather unusual tie-in for Bartell.) He was a member of Seattle's prestigious Rainier Club. And he was a delighted participant in at least one event at the 1909 Alaska-Yukon-Pacific Exposition in Seattle. Bartell was ringmaster at the Elks Day society circus at the exposition on July 28. During the parade just before the circus, one of the horsemen slipped off his steed, ripping off a fuzzy costumed girdle around his waist. The *Seattle Post-Intelligencer* jokingly blamed Bartell for the faux pas in an article the next day, explaining, "He was ringmaster, and he cracked his whip too much."

BELOW: *George Bartell (second from left) and friends show off their catch after a fishing trip, 1930s.*

BOTTOM: *A colorized photo of George Bartell (second from left) on the links at Seattle's Olympic Golf Club in 1929.*

NEW DIRECTIONS AND NEW HEADQUARTERS

Bartell opened a candy factory at 1906 Boren Avenue in 1912 or, more likely, 1913. This was a new direction for the druggist. He'd had success bringing customers to his stores on special occasions with an offer of free candy in exchange for a purchase. But he realized that the company could make much better candy than it could buy and decided to set up his own factory. Though it turned out that Bartell Drugs made little profit from its candy sales, the company benefited in other ways. Customers would stop in for a bite of something sweet, then end up buying other items. The fact that the candy was fresh and locally made (and by a drugstore!) was a bonus.

He put the 1906 Boren building to good use over the next few years for a variety of projects. He moved his headquarters there in 1914. He set up the company warehouse there, and by 1916 had added an ice cream plant. The building became so cramped that in 1916 he enlarged it and added a second floor. A medicinal lab followed, which, in addition to compounding prescriptions, made a number of its own proprietary products, from cold creams to cold remedies, under the Septol label. In 1917 a photo laboratory opened in the building, followed in 1920 by a small store. Though it wasn't Bartell's first store, the company called it Store No. 1 for the next forty-one years.

LEFT TOP: *Bartell's Denny Building store, ca. 1918.*

BOTTOM: *An early view of Bartell Drugs' medicinal lab, believed to date from the 1910s.*

ABOVE RIGHT: *A circa 1905 medicine label for Salvosine, a formula used to treat "catarrh" (congestion), alerted the user that it contained 16 percent alcohol.*

LEFT TOP: *In 1913, Bartell's moved its Ballard store across the street to 5349 Ballard Avenue, where it remained until 1929.*

LEFT BOTTOM: *An interior view of Bartell's first Ballard store at 5344 Ballard Avenue shortly after its 1910 opening.*

OPPOSITE TOP: *Bartell's original headquarters and its Store No. 1 at 1906 Boren Avenue, ca. 1927.*

BOTTOM: *Pharmacist Colin McCord prepares a prescription, 1910s.*

PROHIBITION, MEDICINAL LIQUOR, AND WINE TONICS

On January 1, 1916, Prohibition took effect in Washington State, outlawing the sale and manufacture of liquor. However, the law initially had an exception that allowed for the sale of "medicinal liquor." In Seattle alone, pharmacies sprouted like mushrooms in the rainy season — sixty-five new drugstores opened in the city just in the first three months of 1916. Bartell Drugs likewise sold medicinal liquor, but not for long. State laws were tightened in 1917, and selling medicinal liquor was no longer legal after July 1 of that year until these laws were repealed in 1932. (Bartell's continued to buy and sell alcohol for purposes other than consumption, but it had to post non-beverage alcohol bonds to do so legally.)

Some confusion followed when the National Prohibition Act (also known as the Volstead Act) took effect in 1920. The national act outlawed the sale of alcohol in the United States, but made an exception for medicinal liquor (if state law allowed it, which Washington no longer did). This exception included "wine tonics," which contained up to 22 percent alcohol. These tonics found their way into Washington, and many drugstores, including Bartell Drugs, sold them. Periodically state and local officials would launch a public campaign to take the tonics off the market, claiming that federal laws were being violated. In one such instance in 1929, King County Prosecutor Ewing D. Colvin launched a drive against tonic sales that had the net result of temporarily removing them from window displays and drugstore shelves. Once the heat cooled, the tonics returned.

WORLD WAR I

A number of Bartell Drugs employees enlisted when the United States entered World War I in April 1917. The war slowed the company's expansion, but Bartell did his best to absorb the reduction in workforce. Though most of his key employees and managers were men, he was not averse to hiring women on occasion. In fact, by this time he had hired Edythe Thorp, one of the first female pharmacists in Washington. He may have hired a few more women to fill the gap caused by the war, but took up a lot of the slack himself by working extra hours.

Once again, his health suffered. During a routine checkup his doctor told him to get his affairs in order, because he thought

RIGHT: *George Bartell in the early 1900s.*

Bartell would be dead in six months. The doctor missed the mark by more than thirty years, but on the other hand, Bartell did take him seriously enough to start spending a little more time fishing and golfing.

A Snapshot from 1919

World War I ended in November 1918. By the following year, the company's operations were returning to normal, as the effects of the war slowly ebbed. As 1919 ended, Bartell's medicinal lab was busy producing medications referred to as wets (for liquids,

Patent Medicines

Patent medicines got their name from "letters patent," granted by the English crown to medicine makers for their particular formulas. These patents were first granted in Great Britain in the late seventeenth century, but the name "patent medicine" eventually came to describe all packaged proprietary medicines sold over the counter without a doctor's prescription.

These medicines became more widely used in Great Britain during the eighteenth century and soon found their way to the American colonies. One of the more popular British patent medicines that made it to America was Daffy's Elixir, an alcohol-based laxative. Another was Dr. Bateman's Pectoral Drops, touted to treat rheumatism and other aches and pains. The opium it contained likely did provide effective pain relief.

Patent medicines grew in popularity in the United States during the nineteenth century, reaching their zenith near the end of the century. Lydia Pinkham's Vegetable Compound was well-known. Another popular patent medicine — and one that Bartell Drugs sold in its early years — was swamp root, an herbal remedy said to be good for kidney problems.

Patent medicines were aggressively marketed, and their effectiveness was routinely exaggerated. They were not subject to regulation, and their

contents were not disclosed. This was a problem, because these products often contained dangerous doses of alcohol, opium, morphine, cocaine, and other narcotics. People often took them without understanding what they were taking or even how much they should take. But in an era when medical treatment was still primitive (and largely nonexistent in many rural areas), a lot of people considered patent medicines to be their salvation.

Few patent medicines were ever actually patented in the United States. However, as part of their marketing strategy, many manufacturers developed distinctive trademarks. Again, Lydia Pinkham's Vegetable Compound is a good example. In 1879 Pinkham posed for a photograph that was then used in advertisements of her product. Sales zoomed. In fact, it became so popular that its sales didn't peak until 1925, well after the peak of patent medicine popularity generally.

The passage of the Pure Food and Drug Act in 1906 marked a sea change for the patent medicine industry. Though the act did not prohibit the sale of these products, their ingredients now had to be disclosed and false advertising was prohibited. An even stronger act was passed in 1938. Public attitudes toward patent medicines changed and, for the most part, their sales declined.

such as tincture of iodine) and drys (for solids and powders, such as sodium bicarbonate, more commonly known as baking soda). Manufactured drugs prepared by large pharmaceutical companies were slowly becoming more available but they were far from the norm; more than 80 percent of prescriptions filled in 1919 were compounded by the pharmacist. Though less popular than they had been twenty years earlier, patent medicines were still stocked. Lydia Pinkham's and Peruna were both available in Bartell stores in 1919, as well as another item known simply as "Dynamic Tonic."

A more noticeable change in Bartell drugstores by the end of the decade was a surge in the number of products offered,

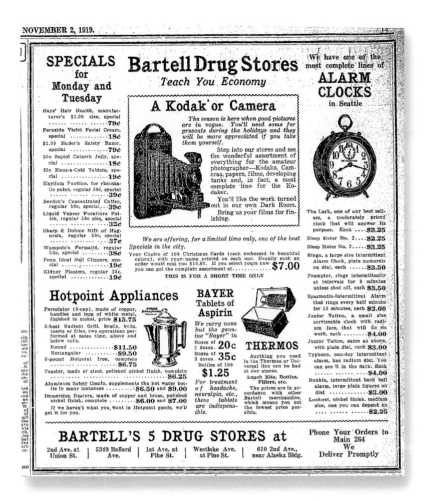

ABOVE: *A Bartell ad in* The Seattle Times *late in 1919 offered Kodaks, clocks, percolators, and more.*

Yet self-medication today continues to be popular with many Americans. All drugstores (and grocery stores, for that matter) offer a huge array of over-the-counter products that can be used for various maladies without a prescription. They aren't called patent medicines, and they're far more regulated than could have been imagined in the nineteenth century. But their diversity and easy availability bring to mind the heyday of patent medicines.

LEFT: *A Lydia Pinkham's vegetable compound ad from World War I in 1917-1918.*

ABOVE: *Various bottles from Bartell's medicinal lab dating from the first half of the twentieth century.*

compared with what the stores had sold at the beginning of the decade. By 1919, you could purchase alarm clocks and cameras at a Bartell drugstore. You could drop off your film there to be developed and leave your camera to be repaired. You could buy irons and toasters, and you could also buy Bartell's candy, in a wide variety of consistencies and flavors. The Bartell store on the corner of 2nd Avenue and Union Street even offered an optical department in 1919, with "glasses fitted and eyes tested scientifically and by a registered optometrist," according to a Bartell ad in *The Seattle Times* that year. It was a taste of what was to come to Bartell stores in the Roaring Twenties.

CHAPTER 3

The Bartell Brand
(1920–1939)

Bartell opened two stores in 1920: one at his office and warehouse location on Boren Avenue, and another late that summer on the southwest corner of 5th Avenue and Pike Street. His eighth store followed in 1921 on the corner of 1st Avenue and Yesler Way, and in 1922 he acquired Store No. 9, located at 1501 2nd Avenue, from Louis F. Swift, who had his own small chain of drugstores in Seattle in the early 1900s. Bartell opened his tenth store in September 1925, on N 45th Street in Wallingford.

By the mid-1920s, this success had caught the eye of one of the country's larger pharmacy chains, the Louis Liggett Company, a subsidiary of the United Drug Company. By 1925, United Drug was a behemoth in the drugstore field. Its Liggett subsidiary alone had more than a thousand stores in the United States, Canada,

and England. (A United Drug franchise, Rexall, was even larger and better known.) In 1925, Liggett began an aggressive buyout campaign of drug companies on the West Coast, and in September the company approached George Bartell with an offer for his ten stores in Seattle.

Bartell at first considered the offer. He traveled to New York City for an unrelated meeting and while there met with representatives of the United Drug Company on October 15. They increased the offer to approximately $1 million. Bartell didn't disclose the exact figure when he was later interviewed, but he did allow that it was a big one: "It was such a big figure, it made me feel sort of sick," he said in an interview with the *Seattle Post-Intelligencer* in November.

NO SALE

Bartell stayed in New York for the next several weeks, and (except for Bartell management and the company's executive board) there appears to have been little public knowledge of the offer. That

OPPOSITE: *An Ovaltine display at one of Bartell's stores in the 1930s. These displays were common in Bartell stores during these years.*
ABOVE: *Bartell delivery truck, 1928.*

changed when he returned to Seattle on the morning of November 12. Two hours after he arrived, Bartell met with his executive board and also invited the managers of all ten of his stores to attend. He put it to a vote — sale or no sale? The result was unanimous: no sale.

There was one more person Bartell approached for input. However, this person wasn't at the meeting; he was in elementary school that morning. In a story that's been proudly handed down in the Bartell family over the years, Bartell talked to his 9-year-old son, George Jr., told him of the offer, and asked for his advice. "I think he knew what he wanted to do," conceded Bartell Jr. years later. "But he came and asked me and said 'what would you like me to do?' I said 'no.'… I think it confirmed what he had already made up his mind to do, but it's interesting that he did approach me on it."

Bartell immediately announced that he had rejected the offer and explained his decision to the *Seattle Post-Intelligencer*:

"I couldn't quite stand to see the stores I have built from one small drug counter, begun down on Jackson Street in 1890, go into the hands of an impersonal outfit with chain stores all over

England, Canada, and America. The managers felt the same way. They've grown up in the business. One of our managers is now selling to the children's children of our first customers. What would a new chain company care about that? Every dollar we have used has been Seattle capital, made from our own stores, put back into new ones. I couldn't sell out."

It was the right decision. The United Drug Company as it existed in the early twentieth century is long gone, though a few scattered stores in the United States still use the Liggett and Rexall names (there are more Rexall stores in Canada, where the brand has a stronger presence). Meanwhile, Bartell Drugs added ten more stores in the next ten years.

THE BARTELL CANDY KITCHEN

Yet Bartell's success was not just about opening stores. Rather, it was rooted in the broadening scope of the company's operations. There were Bartell's food operations, which became an integral part of the company during the 1920s and 1930s, and by 1940 were said to be serving more than ten thousand people a day. All the Bartell drugstores that opened during this time had soda

fountains that provided meals as well as ice cream and soft drinks. Soda fountains were then the rage, providing a social outlet that had been eliminated when saloons closed after Prohibition took effect in Washington in 1916. In addition, upstairs tearooms that also served meals were in some Bartell stores (Store No. 9 on 2nd Avenue and Store No. 16 at Westlake and Pine), and Bartell's Store No. 8 opened a small cafeteria after the company moved the store to a new location on 1st Avenue in 1932. There also was Bartell's photo lab, which was another facet of the company's operations for forty years. But most of all, there was the Bartell Candy Kitchen.

By 1920, the candy kitchen was coming into its own, and it kept growing during the decade. It made a wide variety of candies in various flavors and consistencies. Here's just a handful of selections offered in a 1922 Bartell mail-order catalog (all prices are by the pound, unless otherwise noted):

After Dinner Chocolate Mints, 6 oz. — 25 cents
Assorted Chocolates — $1.00
Dark Chocolate Molasses Mint Chews — 40 cents
Dark Chocolate Raisin Clusters — 60 cents

Dipped Cherries — $1.25
Fruit and Nuts — $1.25
Fudge — 30 cents
Golden Peanut Brittle — 25 cents
Horehound lumps — 30 cents
Lemon drops — 30 cents
Lime Fruit Tablets — 30 cents
Milk Chocolate Fig Chews — 60 cents
Milk Chocolate Honey Nougat — 60 cents
Milk Chocolate Marshmallows — 60 cents
Walnut Patties — 50 cents

ABOVE PHOTOS FROM OPPOSITE LEFT: *The Bartell candy factory at 1906 Boren, ca. 1922.*

Two workers proudly pose in the candy kitchen, ca. 1930.

Cooking candy in the candy factory, ca. 1930.

Two Bartell workers coating chocolate candies in the candy kitchen, ca. 1930.

The Bartell family recalls that Golden Peanut Brittle was one of the best sellers. Also popular were End O' The Week Chocolates, described in a 1923 Bartell ad in *The Seattle Times* as "our best dark and milk-coated chocolates, made fresh each week for Friday and Saturday selling." Other offerings over the years included the Garden Court Frappe, described in a 1924 *Seattle Times* ad as "Not a nougat, not a fudge, but a most delightful, fluffy, creamy foam composed of sugar, whites of eggs, and marshmallow. Maple flavor and loaded with pecans." The same ad also featured Honey Comb Chocolate Chips: "Fresh and crisp with that New Orleans molasses flavor, dipped in dark, sweet chocolate."

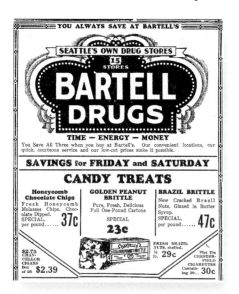

A TON A DAY

In May 1928, the company opened a new building next door to its 1906 Boren Avenue location and moved its office and warehouse to this building at 1916 Boren. The candy kitchen stayed where it was. By this time it was churning out a ton of candy on a typical day, and more than that during the holiday season.

Less than a year later, the candy factory was featured in *The Seattle Times*. In February 1929, the paper wrote about it for a feature in its *National Weekly*, a Sunday magazine. The article gives a vivid snapshot of the Bartell Candy Kitchen as its operations peaked in the last year of the Roaring Twenties:

"Surprisingly light and airy and clean is this factory. The outside walls are virtually all glass. The floors are concrete, scoured until they shine. Tables are metal topped. … Men in immaculate white ducks [pants] preside over shining hammered brass kettles. Girls [young women] in trim uniforms dip chocolates and box and pack them."

In 1929, the factory employed more than twenty people during normal operations, but it doubled the workforce during the weeks before Valentine's Day and between Thanksgiving and New Year's.

THE ART OF CANDY MAKING

The article devoted considerable space to the manufacturing process. The ingredients to make the candies were weighed "correct down to the fraction of an ounce" and then put in a large copper kettle for cooking. Soft candies were cooked at about 240 degrees, while hard candies were cooked at 350. The kettle's contents were monitored by thermometers placed in the boiling liquid. Yet despite all the precision preparation, it was still a subjective call based on the candy maker's eyes and nose when he felt the batch was ready. Once it was, the syrupy mixture was put into a beating machine to cool and then was whipped into the proper consistency. This usually took half an hour or so.

If a fruit candy was being made, it was flavored with natural fruit flavors and crushed fruit — "no artificial flavor is used," the article emphasized. The next step was to send the candy to the chocolate-dipping room, where it was rolled by hand and machine-cut to the desired size. The chocolate-dipping room itself was a sight to behold. Explained the paper:

"Expert chocolate dipping is a revelation to the uninitiated. Girls do the work at almost incredible speed. The molten [chocolate] coating is before them on a marble slab; the fillings on trays at the left. A left hand darts out and palms a filling while the right is coating another. Coated to the proper thickness, the chocolate receives the parting tap that gives it its characteristic uneven top, and another filling flies from the left to the right hand. … Girls coat as much as 200 pounds of chocolate in a single day. No machine that can compete with them has been devised."

The article added that some candies were better when delivered fresh, while others improved if they sat for a few days. Fresh candy was often delivered to Bartell's stores while it was still warm, a company point of pride.

Bartell Drugs continued to use its candies as a marketing tool when it had a holiday sale or special sale, or opened new

LEFT: *A Bartell ad for treats from its candy factory in* The Seattle Times, *March 20, 1930.*

FACING PAGE: *Bartell store window display for licorice candy, ca.1930.*

PHARMACY CHAINS

The first pharmacy chain in the United States, Schlegel Drugstores, opened its first store in Davenport, Iowa, in 1850. A few other chains followed, but their growth was slow for most of the nineteenth century, and they had a relatively small number of stores.

Pharmacy chains began to gradually multiply in the 1890s. This growth accelerated after 1900, led by the United Drug Company, established in 1902 by Louis Liggett. United Drug grew to more than two hundred stores by 1920, but this was small potatoes compared with what came next. Its Rexall franchise flourished to become a staple of thousands of American communities during the twentieth century. In 1958 it was the nation's biggest drug company, with more than eleven thousand franchised stores spread across the country.

Local chains also thrived. G. O. Guy opened his first drugstore in Seattle in 1888 on the corner of Occidental Avenue and Main Street. By the early 1940s there were eleven G. O. Guy stores in the city, and the chain survived until 1987, when it was bought out by Pay'n Save. Another early Seattle chain was Swift's Pharmacy, owned by Louis F. Swift. Swift's first store opened in 1900, and by 1922 the chain had grown to nine or ten stores before swiftly fading from the scene a few years later.

During the 1920s, improvements in technology and transportation helped spur an eruption of pharmacy chains. They galloped across the nation buying smaller stores and chains and building their own stores. Walgreens, founded by Charles Walgreen in 1901, grew from twenty to more than five hundred stores during the 1920s alone. By 1929 there were more than thirty-five hundred chains (companies with three or more pharmacies) in the United States, more than double the number of a decade earlier.

The size and volume of their operations allowed the chains to offer lower prices than their smaller competitors and drove some independent pharmacies out of business. This led to a backlash by both independent pharmacy owners and manufacturers against the chains in the late 1920s. In an attempt to combat their rapid growth, some states passed laws restricting ownership of pharmacies to registered pharmacists, but the U.S. Supreme Court struck down these laws in 1928.

Congress finally confronted the problem in 1937 when it passed the Miller-Tydings Fair Trade Act, allowing manufacturers to control the minimum retail price of various products purchased from a manufacturer for resale. Similar state laws were passed in the 1930s and 1940s, but these laws were widely ignored and all were eventually repealed. Pharmacy chains grew and evolved through the rest of the twentieth century, some expanding into enormous companies. Others experimented — not always successfully — with diversification into retail areas that had not traditionally been part of pharmacy.

Walgreens was the largest retail pharmacy chain in the United States in 2012, with nearly eight thousand stores. While Bartell's isn't the biggest, it has another distinction that means far more to the company: It's the oldest family-owned pharmacy chain with ten or more stores in the country. Bartell's achieved this milestone in 1996 when another family-owned pharmacy chain, Taylor Drugs, was bought out in its 117th year by Rite Aid.

TOP: *George Bartell, pictured in the middle, on a National Association of Chain Drug Stores cruise in 1933.*

LEFT: *Looking north on 2nd Avenue from Yesler Way in 1902. G.O. Guy Drugs, established in Seattle in 1888, dominates the left half of the picture. Bartell's Owl Drugstore, not visible in the picture, is across 2nd Avenue on the right.*

stores. But as the Great Depression took hold in the early 1930s, employment in the candy kitchen ebbed. By late 1932, only about fifteen men and women were working there. Its end quietly followed several years later, in 1937 or 1938.

Window Dressing

Bartell added five more stores during the rest of the 1920s, four in downtown Seattle and another in Seattle's University District. (Aside from a move next door in the 1940s, the U-District store has been at the same spot on the southeast corner of NE 45th Street and University Way NE since 1926, by far the longest Bartell presence at one location.) By this time, most Bartell stores had elaborate window displays. The displays became so important to the company that it opened its own sign-making shop, more formally known as the Window and Sign Department, in 1927. Originally located at 80 Pike Street (directly underneath Bartell's Store No. 3), the shop moved to 1906 Boren Avenue in 1930.

The window displays were serious business. Bartell was known to inspect them while visiting his stores, and he is said to have tipped the store manager a dollar if he saw a particular display he liked. However, the sign shop eventually took care of most of the logistics in preparing the displays. By 1950, nine employees

under the supervision of Display Manager L. P. Daman made all the displays for Bartell stores.

The sign shop had window measurements for all the Bartell stores, and the shop employees built the displays in the shop with an eye on the particular store's window measurements so the display would fit when it was taken to the store to be set up. The shop artists built, trimmed, and painted backgrounds and lettering for the signs, and they created any other artwork necessary for the window displays. The goal was to change each display in each store once every two weeks. (This was quite a job by 1950, when Bartell Drugs had grown to twenty-one stores.) As times changed and Bartell Drugs reinvented itself in the 1960s and 1970s, the displays specific to individual windows faded away. However, Bartell's still made window signs for its stores and ran a print shop that prepared these signs until 2011, when the shop finally vanished into history.

Changes in Pharmacy

Products sold in Bartell drugstores rapidly changed during the 1920s. On the pharmaceutical side, the trend toward physicians prescribing more manufacturer-produced drugs accelerated. Advances in chemistry created new drugs whose quality was more dependable, and their contents could be measured more precisely than pharmacist-compounded prescriptions. Because these drugs could be manufactured more uniformly, physicians (and pharmacists) could now more accurately assess how well a prescription worked. Though compounded prescriptions still made up a sizable majority of prescriptions filled during the 1920s, the use of manufactured drugs was becoming more common.

At the same time, the decline in the popularity of patent medicines accelerated. By 1929, Lydia Pinkham's and Peruna had disappeared from Bartell ads (though Bartell's continued to carry Lydia Pinkham's for many years afterward), but you could still get a pint of witch hazel for 29 cents, only 4 cents more than it cost at a Bartell store in 1900. Cod liver oil also was still a popular item on Bartell shelves, to the chagrin of children with well-meaning

Bartell window display, ca. 1930.

mothers. Aspirin became more widely used in the 1920s and was a popular item in Bartell stores by 1929.

FACE CREAM, FLASHLIGHTS, AND FLOOR WAX

The variety and number of products available at Bartell Drugs soared during the 1920s. National figures show the strength of this surge: In 1880, twenty-seven hundred different products and sizes of products were sold in the pharmacy market nationally. By 1916, this figure had grown to thirty-eight thousand, and it reached sixty thousand by 1933. Many of these new products were cosmetics, reflecting the increase of women using makeup. By 1929, women could buy face cream, lipstick, eye shadow, and even a perfumed liquid called Vanish (said to remove "surplus hair" quickly and easily) at a Bartell Drugs. Men could buy shaving lotion, razors, cologne, and hair tonics.

You could buy flashlights and floor wax, saxophones and silver polish, and tennis balls and toasters at a Bartell drugstore in 1929. That Christmas you could not only buy your Christmas cards at Bartell's but the lights for your Christmas tree, too. You could buy Bartell's French Cleaner, a fabric cleaner made by the company that was popular with customers. And, in at least one store in the autumn of 1929, Bartell Drugs offered the "Olympic Oscillator," a vibrating belt machine, on sale for $42.50. The ad for the machine was hard to miss: An attractive young woman, clad in shockingly short shorts, modeled the oscillator in the display window of Store No. 9 one Friday evening in November. There is no word on how many oscillators were sold, though the display was probably effective at attracting customers, at least on the masculine side.

Bartell seemed to enjoy bringing in live talent to help stimulate business. For example, there was a particular emphasis in the United States during the 1920s and 1930s on promoting regularity. Bartell Drugs carried a number of brands of laxatives to meet the need, such as Serutan (said to tone up sluggish intestinal action) and Sargon. For several months during 1929, Bartell let a Sargon representative meet the public in his drugstore near Pike Place Market to sing the praises of the "revolutionary new medicine." Glowing testimonials (resembling actual newspaper articles) for the soft pills appeared for several months in *The Seattle Times*, always ending with the line that the "special Sargon representative"

LEFT: *Bartell's French Cleaner.*

BELOW: *A model displays the Olympic Oscillator in a "live" window display at Bartell's Store No. 9 on the corner of 2nd Avenue and Pike Street, November 22, 1929.*

FACING PAGE, LEFT: *A Bartell Drugs ad in the* Seattle Shopping News *from 1936.*

RIGHT: *Bartell Drugs held a special dinner on November 4, 1938, to honor its Asian employees. George Bartell is seated in the middle, while George Bartell Jr. appears second from the right.*

was at the Bartell drugstore at 1st Avenue and Pike Street meeting hundreds of people. An exaggeration perhaps, but it doubtlessly did bring in more customers.

Dodging the Great Depression

The United States was spiraling into the Great Depression as the 1930s began. The profound and protracted economic collapse made the depression of the 1890s look like a mild downturn. Yet, despite the Depression, Bartell Drugs continued to prosper. This was for several reasons. The company didn't carry much debt, enabling it to ride out the economic storm. But the storm largely bypassed Bartell Drugs in any event. Bartell stores stocked many inexpensive essentials — both medication and retail products — that people needed, no matter how bad the economy got. And George Bartell's personal touch with his customers worked. People liked him and liked coming to his stores. Growth at Bartell's not only didn't slow in the early 1930s; the company continued to expand, opening five stores in the first half of the decade.

Bartell Drugs had a policy of buying as many products made or grown in the Northwest as it could in order to emphasize the local nature of its business. During the Depression

it stepped up this policy. In one instance, Bartell stores sold Washington-grown apples at cost "just to boost the industry and help the orchard growers out during a pretty difficult period," Bartell explained in a subsequent interview. Likewise, when Washington dairy farmers were faced with a surplus of milk in the summer of 1937, Bartell Drugs launched a monthlong "milk drive" to sell more milk at its lunch counters.

This product loyalty was returned by Bartell's customers, who shopped in droves at its stores. By the mid-1930s, the company's retail sales topped $2.5 million annually, and its stores filled nearly ten thousand prescriptions a month. Bartell Drugs had almost five hundred people on its payroll, providing significant opportunities not only to pharmacists but to clerks and soda jerks during a time when there were few opportunities to be had.

The Personal Touch

George Bartell had developed a habit in the company's earliest years of visiting each of his stores regularly and chatting with its employees to show his interest in and appreciation for their work. But while he kept an eagle eye on his stores, he favored a hands-off approach with their managers. He explained his philosophy in a 1930 interview with Leo Lassen of the *Seattle Star*: "You have to learn to trust other people to succeed in business. I don't do

anything. I never interfere with my managers; each is responsible for his unit. I like to develop my own help." This tradition of personal store visits by Bartell family members was handed down to Bartell's son George Jr., and then to his grandson, George D. Bartell, though most of these visits are now made during the Christmas season.

A nattily attired and confident Bartell photo courier with a load in front of a downtown Bartell store, 1930s.

Photo labs were already in business in Seattle when Bartell Drugs opened its lab in 1917 with one developer and a part-time assistant. However, George Bartell took a good idea and expanded on it, and the expansion was rapid: Five years later, fifteen employees were working in the lab. By the time it was the subject of a *Seattle Post-Intelligencer* article in 1932, the photo lab boasted six modern printing machines and an automatic film-developing machine (the developing machine was a big deal in 1932).

Bartell Drugs developed about nine hundred rolls of film a day in 1932. And customers could count on having their pictures back fast. Those who brought in film by 12:30 p.m. could pick up pictures by 5 p.m., and film brought in between 12:30 and 4:30 p.m. would be developed by

Lassen in his article went on to describe the active and personable Bartell:

> "Bartell, in middle life, prefers worsted business suits, wears quiet ties and glasses. He speaks rather hurriedly and is a ready conversationalist. He loves out-door life and prefers the company of young people. Bartell has just returned from a week's fishing in the Cascades and is bronzed by the sun. He likes to pack into trackless streams. … There is nothing fussy as an executive about Bartell. He had his fishing paraphernalia packed in his private office and spent half an hour demonstrating its various uses."

Bartell had remarried in 1920, shortly after he and Beatrice divorced. Little is known of his third wife, Zedna, with one exception — she was twenty-five years Bartell's junior. The 1930 United States Census shows them living in a house on 1st Avenue N on

BARTELL'S PHOTO LABORATORY

noon the next day. To ensure speedy service, Bartell's hired a motorcycle messenger, who spent his days zipping through Seattle between the lab and the Bartell stores. He stopped at each store at least three times a day.

Bartell's photo lab also offered an airbrush colorizing process for pictures. This process took an ordinary black and white photograph and turned it into a color photograph. (Color film wasn't widely used until after World War II.) Though it was sometimes possible to tell the photograph had been retouched, the colorizing still added a nice touch to a personal or family portrait.

During the late 1930s, Bartell's had a monthly "menu print competition" of its favorite photographs. The company selected what it felt was the best photograph out of the tens of thousands it developed each month, and, with the owner's permission, reprinted it on all its menu covers for a month. The photo contests continued over the years, though they later changed. By the 1950s, contests were held weekly. Four winning photographs were selected, and, with the owners' approval, they were enlarged and displayed in all Bartell stores during the following week.

The lab continued to thrive into the 1950s under the management of L. L. Connell, who had worked in the lab since it opened. But by this time its days were numbered. The growing popularity of color film made Bartell's black-and-white photo developing operation obsolete. It was impractical to upgrade the lab to handle color processing, so it instead closed in the late 1950s.

But this was not the end of photo processing at Bartell Drugs. Today, you can walk into many Bartell Drug stores and have a print from a film camera developed within an hour in one of the photo-processing machines in the store. Or you can print your own digitally stored pictures in just a few minutes at one of Bartell's digital print centers. You can even e-mail your pictures to a Bartell store, where they will be printed and ready for pickup in an hour.

A Bartell photo receipt, 1935.

PROHIBITION AND MEDICINAL LIQUOR

Before Prohibition became effective in Washington on January 1, 1916, one could buy liquor in drugstores. It was generally found in the patent medicines that the stores commonly stocked, though this wasn't medicinal liquor. Medicinal liquor was regular liquor sold by prescription for medicinal purposes. And when Prohibition first took effect, there was an exception in the law that allowed for the sale of medicinal liquor in the state's drugstores under a permit system. The day state Prohibition took effect, Bartell Drugs held a board of trustees meeting where it was agreed that its stores would carry a supply of liquor.

It didn't last. In February 1917, Governor Ernest Lister signed House Bill 4, otherwise known as the bone-dry law, which prohibited the importation of liquor into the state. Before the new state law even took effect, Congress passed similar federal legislation that outlawed the shipment of liquor into any state that had dry laws as of July 1, 1917. Since liquor wasn't manufactured in Washington, this cut off the pipeline for alcohol into the state and marked the end of legal medicinal liquor in Washington for the next fifteen years.

National Prohibition took effect in 1920, though it too allowed for the sale of medicinal liquor in states that did not have their own laws prohibiting it. This was supposed to be a moot point in Washington, but medicinal liquor still found its way into the state's drugstores under the guise of "wine tonics," which contained up to 22 percent alcohol.

The struggle continued through the 1920s and into the 1930s, but it eventually became apparent that Prohibition had failed. In November 1932, Washington voters passed Initiative 61, repealing the state's bone-dry law. Local ordinances that contained their own restrictions were also repealed. This paved the way for the return of medicinal liquor into the state, subject to the federal restriction of one pint every ten days per patient.

Tacoma was the first city in the state to provide medicinal liquor in its drugstores, where it was available by December 17. In Seattle it took a little longer. Doctors and druggists were required to have a permit to prescribe and sell liquor, and they inundated the Bureau of Industrial Alcohol with so many applications that the bureau was overwhelmed. The applications were finally approved just in time for New Year's Eve, and liquor hit Seattle drugstore shelves on December 31, 1932.

The number of Seattleites suffering from colds and other maladies surged. People who normally avoided the doctor suddenly decided it was time for a visit. Sympathetic doctors had little problem prescribing a pint to their patients, who then rushed to the nearest drugstore. To say it was a Happy New Year in Seattle is an understatement. Despite their "illnesses," Seattleites partied.

Bartell Drugs stocked liquor in its stores, albeit reluctantly, because this created its own problems. In May 1933, Bartell's Wallingford store was broken into and thieves escaped with ten pints of medicinal whiskey and 175 cartons of cigarettes — but they took no money. A similar break-in later that year at the Bartell store at 2nd Avenue and Pike Street netted the burglars six quarts of whiskey but again, no money (although in that particular burglary, the yeggs did try to break open the safe).

National Prohibition was repealed in its entirety in December 1933, eliminating the need for medicinal liquor. Liquor officially disappeared from Washington drugstores three months later when the state took over hard-liquor sales. But in 2011, Washington voters voted to privatize state liquor sales, and booze returned to the retail shelves of Washington drugstores in June 2012. It's not medicinal liquor. But a wag might call it such.

Serial No. RF83580 Proof 100

Kind and Quantity Whiskey Pt.

For G. Hausen

1426 Market

Dr. W.T. Christensen

Directions Wineglassful 3 times daily.

No. Date 7-14-33

BARTELL DRUG STORE NO. 4
2225 Market St.

PRODUCED BY D. K. WEISKOPF
DISTILLERY NO. 9—DISTRICT OF KENTUCKY
PRODUCED PRIOR TO SEPTEMBER 8TH, 1917

CAUTION NOTICE This bottle has been filled and stamped under the provisions of the Act of Congress approved March 3, 1897, entitled "An Act to allow the bottling of distilled spirits in Bond," and under the provisions of the Act approved February 17, 1922. Any person who shall reuse this bottle for the purpose of containing distilled spirits without removing and destroying the stamp affixed to this bottle, or who shall re-use the stamp affixed to this bottle, will be liable for each such offence to a fine of not less than one hundred nor more than one thousand dollars, and to imprisonment for not more than two years.

FOR MEDICINAL PURPOSES ONLY
Sale or use for other purposes will cause heavy penalties to be inflicted
BOTTLED IN BOND at Distillery No. 4—23rd District of Pennsylvania

A prescription label on the back of a pint of legal medicinal whiskey, sold at Bartell's Ballard store on July 14, 1933.

Queen Anne Hill but offers little additional information about Zedna other than that she was born in Oregon in 1894. The couple had no children together. In 1934, Zedna divorced George Bartell on the grounds that he neglected her for his business. He did not contest the divorce.

THE TRIANGLE STORE

In July 1935, Bartell leased a site for another new store at 401 Pine Street (where Westlake Park is today) in downtown Seattle. The site had been the location of the Plaza Hotel for the preceding thirty years, but the hotel was quickly torn down later that summer and a new building built that fall. The two-story, fireproof building had a marble exterior and non-rusting metal trim, and its distinctive triangular shape almost immediately earned it the nickname "the triangle store."

Over the next half century this store would be known as Bartell Drugs' flagship store. A tearoom with pleasant furnishings and a great view offered meals on the building's second floor. The first floor housed the soda fountain and the prescription department. Other merchandise also was sold on the first floor and in the basement. (By 1950, the basement store was a "self-service" store, a nod toward the future.) A remodeling job in the late 1940s expanded the store's total area on its three floors to more than thirteen thousand square feet, making it one of Bartell's largest stores up to that time.

Given its central location in the heart of downtown Seattle, the store became the highest-volume store in the company for many years during the middle of the century. It played a key role in the company's survival during the 1950s and 1960s, and became a training ground for new employees. The store was managed in its early years by C. J. Moore, and in the early 1960s Sanford Barnes became manager. Barnes, a plain-speaking, no-nonsense

RIGHT TOP: *Bartell's triangle store as seen from 4th Avenue, 1937.*

CENTER: *Bartell's triangle store tearoom.*

BOTTOM: *The soda fountain at Bartell's triangle store, 1930s.*

southerner, trained a number of Bartell employees who went on to the upper echelons of the company's management. These included George D. Bartell and Jean Bartell.

But in the 1980s, a dispute arose between Bartell Drugs and its landlord over the terms of Bartell's lease. The dispute went to court, and Bartell's lost. As a result, the company closed the triangle store in April 1984 and moved it to another location downtown. The building was demolished as part of construction of the Westlake Mall project, which was completed in 1988.

GEORGE BARTELL JR.

George Bartell Jr. had grown up with his mother and sister in the house on 11th Avenue W on Queen Anne Hill. He was by nature a quiet, reserved child, and his parents' divorce likely exacerbated his natural reticence. He was bright, and graduated as an honor student from Queen Anne High School in 1934. He then went to the University of Washington and took core classes with an emphasis on economics and business during his first year.

George Bartell Jr. was not eagerly waiting in the wings for his opportunity to take over the company as he finished his first year of college. That's not to say he wasn't interested. After all, he had advised his father to turn down the million-dollar offer from the Louis Liggett Company to purchase Bartell Drugs in 1925. He also saw his father regularly as he grew up and occasionally accompanied him on fishing trips, where the two no doubt talked shop.

And in his senior year of high school, he accompanied the elder Bartell on a National Association of Chain Drug Stores convention cruise from New York City to Nassau and Havana. He met Charles Walgreen, the founder of Walgreens drugstores, and listened to him discuss the need to adopt fair trade laws to reduce deep discounting of drugstore items. (Such a law was later enacted. It was an ironic sequel to the senior Bartell's fight with the Seattle Drug Trust in the early 1900s to prevent price-setting.) The trip left a big impression on the young Bartell.

George Bartell Sr. was 66 years old in the summer of 1935, several years past the life expectancy of the day. Because of this and because of the health scares he'd had over the years, he talked to his son about joining the company. George Bartell Jr. would probably have been just as happy to stay in college, but he was strongly influenced by his father. On August 5, 1935, he started as a warehouseman for Bartell Drugs, earning the princely sum of $14.50 a week.

He rose quickly through the ranks. In 1936, he transferred to the new triangle store at Westlake and Pine and worked as a stock boy and part-time clerk. He next moved to the company's headquarters at 1916 Boren Avenue and was put in charge of purchasing candy and tobacco. (After that stint, he didn't enjoy candy. Likewise, he never smoked.) In 1938, he was also put in charge of supervising the design, construction, and remodeling of the company's stores. As a result of this experience, he developed a keen interest in the design and construction of the stores, and for most of the next fifty years he was involved in determining the layout of many of Bartell's new and remodeled stores.

On September 27, 1939, George Bartell Jr. was elected president of the Bartell Drug Company. He actually replaced his mother, who resigned the presidency and became vice president. (In 1941, his sister Amy Bartell Meakin would become a second vice president of the company.) George Bartell Sr., who had been vice president, became secretary. However, the senior Bartell remained an active presence in the company for most of the next seventeen years, until his death in 1956. Indeed, this presence to some degree stymied the younger Bartell's pursuing his own plans for the company. But as the 1930s segued into the 1940s, it would become a moot point. As Bartell Jr. would later write in his memoir: "World War II came along to change a lot of plans."

George Bartell Jr., ca. 1936.

№ 7

№ 11

№ 8

№ 12

Bartell's Store No. 7 ~ southwest corner of 5th Avenue and Pike Street, 1922.
Bartell's Store No. 11 ~ University Way in Seattle's University District, 1929.
Bartell's Store No. 8 ~ southwest corner of 1st Avenue and Yesler Way, 1921.
Bartell's Store No. 12 ~ Seattle's Orpheum Theater, 1928.

CHAPTER 4

War and Stagnation
(1940–1955)

The 1940s got off to a quiet start for the Bartell Drug Company. Its fiftieth anniversary that spring passed without fanfare. Probably the biggest event of 1940 for Bartell Drugs was the opening of its twenty-second store in late June. The attractive, striking building was located at 7804 Aurora Avenue N in Seattle, and was designed by George Bartell Jr. A *Seattle Times* article on June 30, 1940, said the new store incorporated "scores of recently developed features of modern drug merchandising" but didn't elaborate, with one exception. The store had a sunken soda fountain, said to enable employees to provide faster service.

The new store was part of the company's plan to modernize and upgrade its stores. This had begun in 1935, and accelerated in 1938 when George Bartell Jr. became involved in the design, construction, and remodeling of Bartell stores. He quickly developed an interest and aptitude in this area. With input from other company executives, he helped design a new store on California Avenue in West Seattle that the company opened (with, of course, an introductory sale) in September 1938. To that point, it was one of the largest stores in the Bartell chain. It had thirty-five hundred square feet, and a special refrigeration unit to store serums and antitoxins.

By the time the new Aurora Avenue store opened in June 1940, Bartell Drugs was remodeling two more stores, including its store on the corner of 1st Avenue and Marion Street. When the remodel was finished in November, the store offered the Bartell Buffet Grill, a cafeteria (and soda fountain) with seating for 258 people. Patrons could sit at the lunch counter, slide into a booth, or opt for one of two dining rooms (though one initially was reserved for small groups).

Despite wars raging in Europe and Asia, the company looked forward to a prosperous Christmas in 1940. "Yessir," exclaimed George Bartell Sr. when he was interviewed by *The Seattle Times* in November, "it's going to be a great Christmas this year … we are

OPPOSITE: *Bartell's Store No. 22 on Aurora Avenue shortly after its June 1940 opening.*

ABOVE: *Bartell's 1940 gift catalog cover.*

looking forward to the greatest volume of Christmas buying ever." But this would be the last Christmas for a long time that Bartell Drugs would be able to look forward with such optimism. No one knew it yet, but the company was at a peak. By Christmas 1941, the United States would be embroiled in World War II. The war would trigger a chain reaction that would profoundly impact the Bartell Drug Company.

WORLD WAR II'S WALLOP

The war had a far greater impact on Bartell Drugs than World War I had had twenty-five years earlier. Bartell's was a much larger company than it had been in World War I, but as had been the case in World War I, many of its employees either volunteered or were drafted into this new war. This included George Bartell Jr., who entered the U.S. Army in May 1942 and served for nearly four years. The resulting manpower shortage was more severe than it had been in World War I, lasted longer, and was more difficult for Bartell Drugs to overcome. The company hired more women to fill in, but this didn't entirely solve the problem. The personnel shortage continued to plague Bartell's until after the war ended late in the summer of 1945.

Employees of Japanese heritage were disproportionately affected. During the 1920s and 1930s, many Bartell stores had Japanese stockers, dishwashers, and janitors. The company honored these employees for their service in November 1938 with a special "Japanese dinner" that was attended by both George Bartell Sr. and Jr. and other company executives. By the time the war broke out there were about sixty Japanese (or Japanese descendants) working for the company, out of about 650 employees company-wide. However, early in the war all employees of Japanese ancestry were relocated to internment camps outside of Washington. None of these employees is believed to have returned to work for Bartell Drugs after the war.

During the war many items in the United States were rationed, and the manufacture of consumer goods took a back seat to military production. In anticipation of shortages of these goods, the company began stockpiling inventory so it could have as large a supply as possible on hand. Bartell's spent so much on stockpiling inventory that it led to cash-flow problems. In a few instances, this resulted in the company's inability to pay salaries to some employees. As the war continued, the company actually was forced to borrow funds to be able to buy more inventory.

But the war dragged on. So did the shortage of employees, and so did rationing. Gasoline was rationed, which meant that many Bartell customers had to plan their trips to the drugstore. It was now more difficult for a customer to drop in on a whim — something that Bartell's had often counted on in the past to boost business. As these and other war-related issues set in, the company began to lose money.

By the end of 1943, the company was unable to raise sufficient working capital to meet its needs. If this wasn't unprecedented, it certainly was the first time it had happened since Bartell's early years.

Bartell's tailored its window displays to the times, as this display featured during World War II shows, ca. 1942.

George Bartell Jr.'s War Years

In May 1942, George Bartell Jr. was drafted into the U.S. Army. (His father ran the company in his absence.) He was inducted at Fort Lewis, and then sent to Camp Crowder, Missouri, for basic training. He also was given a battery of tests at Camp Crowder to determine how his particular skills could best be used, and scored high in intelligence testing. As a result, he was sent to Camp Murphy, Florida, for radar training. Radar was fairly new in the early 1940s, and the word itself was still such a secret that the servicemen were required to call it by a technical name, pulse goniometry.

Bartell was soon transferred to Fort Monmouth, New Jersey, for officer training in the Signal Corps. After graduating in the winter of 1943 as a second lieutenant, he was assigned to work in the headquarters of the Alaska Communications System at the Federal Building in downtown Seattle. He was amazed at the freedom he had with this assignment. He was even able to live at home with his mother. But he was a temporary pool officer subject to reassignment, and after nearly a year in Seattle, he received orders transferring him to the Corps of Engineers.

Early in 1944, he found himself bound for Guadalcanal, an island in the South Pacific that had been the scene of bitter U.S.–Japanese fighting earlier in the war. He wrote in his memoir that the soldiers learned "pidgin English" en route across the Pacific. They tried it out not long after their arrival, when two natives wearing breechcloths happened by. No doubt thinking they were clever, the Americans greeted the natives: "We come long way." One of the natives retorted, "The hell you say."

ABOVE: *George Bartell Jr. during his Army years, ca. 1944.*
RIGHT: *George Bartell Jr., in the middle, taking a break in the South Pacific, ca. 1945.*

Bartell and his unit were in charge of the Guadalcanal water supply. After about six months there, he was transferred to Luzon Island in the Philippines to prepare for an anticipated invasion of Japan. As part of this preparation, he was issued a big book of maps and aerial photographs of Japan, which George D. Bartell still has. However, the Japanese surrender in September 1945 made an invasion unnecessary.

Though the war was over, Bartell's military service was not. For several months after the war ended, he served as part of the occupation force in the city of Nagoya, a large seaport on the eastern shore of Japan's Honshu Island. While he was in Nagoya, he had time to visit the surrounding city and countryside on Sundays and later said he enjoyed the experience.

Bartell was discharged from the Army in March 1946, having attained the rank of captain. He returned to Seattle and resumed his duties as president of Bartell Drugs. He didn't discuss his war experience much, but when he did, he often pointed out that he was never exposed to enemy fire during his four years in the Army.

Hours for some stores were cut, and some stores began closing on Sunday. Bartell Drugs actually lost money in 1945, something that would have been unimaginable five years earlier.

WAR ENDS, BUT PROBLEMS CONTINUE

The war ended in 1945, but the shortages and problems created by the war did not. Price controls on some consumer goods continued for several more years, limiting the company's ability to raise prices as needed. Even after price controls were lifted, Bartell's was stymied by the Miller-Tydings Fair Trade Act, which gave manufacturers the ability to control the minimum retail price of various products purchased from the manufacturer for resale. This included certain cosmetics and over-the-counter drugs. Though the law eventually came to be largely ignored — and was repealed in 1975 — it prevented Bartell Drugs from lowering its prices to meet competition from other retailers who ignored the law.

Though the company had some good years in the late 1940s, those mainly served to recoup earlier losses. The robust growth that Bartell's had enjoyed in the 1920s and 1930s did not return. After opening its Aurora Avenue store in 1940, the company only opened one more store during the entire decade, on Mercer Street in 1948. At the same time, competition from new self-service stores, such as Pay'n Save and Payless, lured customers away from Bartell Drugs. Moreover, many of the younger managers who had worked for Bartell's before the war pursued other opportunities after the war, leaving a management team in place that was older and either unable or unwilling to see the need for change, much less make recommendations for it. To add fuel to the slowly expanding fire, Bartell's union employees began demanding higher raises. These issues would only intensify in the 1950s.

RIGHT TOP: *A look inside Store No. 19 on Roosevelt Way in the 1950s. Manager William Pappe is smiling at the camera.*

BELOW: *A page from a 1940 Bartell gift catalog offered a broad range of gifts.*

OPPOSITE TOP: *George Bartell at his country home near Meadowdale in Snohomish County, 1940s.*

BELOW: *Betty and George Bartell Jr. on their wedding day, Seattle, December 1, 1948.*

MANUFACTURED DRUGS AND SELF-SERVICE DRUGSTORES

Pharmacy itself was changing as the 1940s ended, not just in the products that were sold, but also in how they were sold. Compounded prescriptions had not disappeared entirely by 1949 — indeed, Bartell's medicinal lab was still in operation in a part of the building at 1916 Boren Avenue — but they were less prevalent than they had been in earlier years. In a 1943 interview with the *Seattle Star*, George Bartell Sr. remarked that he sometimes doubted that a modern pharmacist could compound some of the "shotgun prescriptions" that he had filled fifty years earlier. Manufacturer-produced drugs, with their dependable uniformity and quality, were taking their place.

Meanwhile, self-service drugstores were starting to establish themselves by the late 1940s, providing considerable competition to Bartell Drugs, which was still very much a full-service operation. Self-service drugstores typically were larger and had lower shelving that allowed customers to select a product rather than requiring a clerk to get the product for them. Self-service was faster and more streamlined for the customer and less labor-intensive for the store owner. It would soon become the norm, but Bartell Drugs was slow to recognize the trend. Its transition to self-service was one of the few areas in retail where it was behind the curve.

GEORGE BARTELL JR. MARRIES

There was good news for the Bartell family in 1948 when George Bartell Jr. married. He had dated Elizabeth "Betty" Bogue for perhaps two or three years before he entered the Army in 1942. Born in Nebraska in 1911, Betty Bogue had moved to Seattle at age 5, where her father, Horace, was an early partner in Ernst Hardware. She graduated from Garfield High School and attended the University of Washington, but was forced to drop out during the Depression when her father lost his interest in the hardware company. The family swapped some Seattle real estate holdings for a dairy ranch in Winthrop, and the family went broke. The Bogues moved to Winthrop and scraped out a living farming. Betty eventually returned to Seattle and met George Bartell Jr. through mutual friends at Kellogg & Son. (Kellogg & Son was a cabinet shop in Seattle's Georgetown that prepared all of Bartell's store fixtures in

RIGHT: *Bartell's sixtieth anniversary was prominently featured in a series of articles in* The Seattle Times *on March 26, 1950.*

FAR RIGHT ABOVE: *Advertising manager Ed Arbow designs an ad commemorating Bartell's sixtieth anniversary inside Bartell's sign shop, 1950.*

RIGHT BELOW: *Supervisor Eve Comstock (right) training members of Bartell's cosmetics department, 1950.*

the late 1930s and early 1940s, when the company was modernizing many of its stores.)

The couple resumed their relationship after he returned from overseas in 1946, and were married on December 1, 1948. George Bartell Sr. objected to the wedding, partly because the bride was five years older than his son. The senior Bartell — whose own marriages indicated a penchant for younger women — argued that a man's wife should be the younger partner in the marriage. He also was unjustly wary of Betty Bogue's motives because of her family's financial setbacks during the Depression, and demanded that she sign a prenuptial agreement. Despite his issues, the new couple went on to have a happy life together. They settled into Seattle's Magnolia neighborhood and eventually had three children: George D. in 1951, Jean in 1953, and Robert in 1954.

SIXTIETH ANNIVERSARY CELEBRATION

The 1950s started with a bang for Bartell Drugs. The company had a gala sixtieth anniversary celebration the last week of March. As part of the celebration, Bartell's ran a series of articles in an entire

Sunday section of *The Seattle Times* on March 26, 1950, that provided a vivid picture of the company, its operations, and its stores.

As the 1950s began, Bartell Drugs operated twenty-one stores. The company had more than five hundred employees and an annual payroll of nearly $1.5 million. Many of these employees had worked for Bartell's for thirty and forty years. The company employed fifty-three registered pharmacists, and claimed this was more than any other Pacific Northwest firm. Bartell Drugs had filled more than five million prescriptions in its sixty-year history.

But the Bartell's of 1950 was selling far more than just drugs. There was its photo lab, which served thousands of customers yearly. There were its food operations, serving upward of ten thousand people a day in its restaurants and at its fountains. There were its purchasing operations, which in 1950 were labor-intensive. That year Bartell Drugs stocked more than forty thousand items in its stores. In an era before a computer tracked what sold well and what did not, it was up to the merchandise manager and his team to make this judgment. The manager and his team dealt with literally thousands of suppliers, and they had to review countless items, from drugs to magazines, to determine what would sell at Bartell stores.

The company even had a cosmetics department. In the early 1950s it employed fifty-two cosmeticians, supervised by the aptly named Eve Fairness (otherwise known as Eve Comstock). These were not women who simply provided a few makeup tips. All of them regularly took training courses to keep current on the latest in cosmetics and fashion.

George Bartell Sr.'s Later Years

In some ways, George Bartell's senior years weren't that different from his earlier ones. He kept working right up until nearly the end. In a 1930 interview with Leo Lassen of the *Seattle Star*, he'd explained, "I'll never quit. Why should I? These stores are my biggest kick in life." And they were.

In his later years Bartell maintained a one-room apartment on the second floor of the company offices on Boren, a spartan room with a sink. He often walked from his apartment to have breakfast at the Bartell store on 2nd Avenue and Pike Street, and then later the same day walked to the triangle store for lunch and back for dinner, regardless of the weather. No doubt he stopped to chat people up along the way.

Bartell also had a country home in a small valley north of Meadowdale (located in what today is the northern fringes of the city of Edmonds, near Meadowdale Beach Park). It was a plain but pleasant — and roomy for a bachelor — two-story house, with woods and a nearby creek. He cut trees for firewood and kept a garden of vegetables and flowers. This was not a small garden. A 1951 article in *The Seattle Times* claimed it had thousands of bulbs. Whatever the number, it produced enough flowers that Bartell frequently decorated his stores with them.

Presumably, he still enjoyed fly fishing, though there's less mention of it in the accounts of his last years, in contrast to his earlier years. And he

George Bartell, Amy Bartell Meakin, and George Bartell Jr. at a Bartell Drugs manager's dinner commemorating the company's sixtieth anniversary, 1950.

gave up golf entirely in the 1930s, admitting that he was "always all over the course except on the fairway" — but then claiming he quit only because his golf club reorganized. He liked taking in a good game of base-ball, and enjoyed the card game of bridge. He also was an avid reader. But it was his stores that kept drawing him back. Even at age 85, he was still putting in full days in his office when he was in town. "I'll retire when I'm flat on my back and can't get up," he said in a 1954 newspaper interview.

He never did retire. He spoke at the company's sixty-fifth anniversary dinner in Seattle in the spring of 1955, and everyone assumed he would do the same at the sixty-sixth. But in March 1956, just as the anniversary approached, Bartell fell seriously ill, perhaps with pneumonia. He lingered in the hospital for about a week, and died on Friday afternoon, March 30, 1956 (by coincidence Good Friday), at Doctors Hospital in Seattle. At the time of his death, he'd become known as the oldest operator of a drugstore chain in the country.

And the company did not limit itself to selling in its stores. Since at least 1920, Bartell Drugs had had a mail-order department that paid postage for items shipped within Washington, with the exception of cigarettes. The company had customers from far outside the state, though. In fact, it had customers from far outside the United States: By 1950, Bartell Drugs had shipped orders to dozens of countries worldwide, among them Sweden, Greece, Turkey, and India.

A New Store at Northgate

In April 1950, Seattle's Northgate Shopping Mall opened. Billed as the nation's first regional shopping center to be called a mall, Northgate generated considerable excitement at its opening. It was the wave of the future. Seeing the opportunity, George Bartell Sr. opened a drugstore in the mall in May 1951. The opening came with the usual flair: It was noted in the press, and all Bartell stores offered a three-day sale in recognition of the new store. Its opening was even topped off with a special square-dancing event in the mall parking lot.

Shipments to the store were delivered to a tunnel that ran underneath the mall. A conveyor belt transported the merchandise up from the tunnel to the store itself.

The store had a food bar and a fountain serving drinks with names like Purple Cow (vanilla ice cream and grape juice) and Cool Florida Limeade. The fountain was an instant hit, and earned the distinction of lasting longer than any of the other Bartell soda fountains in its twenty-plus stores. As soda fountains declined in popularity in the 1960s and 1970s, Bartell Drugs began closing them, one by one. But the Northgate fountain, a testament to an earlier time, remained open until 1982.

FACING PAGE CLOCKWISE FROM TOP: *Celebrating the opening of Bartell's new Northgate store with a square dance in the adjacent parking lot, May 1951.*

Northgate store opening in May 1951.

A two-page ad in The Seattle Times *on May 15, 1951, celebrated the opening of Bartell's new store at Seattle's Northgate Mall.*

A rainy-day shot of the entrance to Bartell Drugs' Northgate store not long after its opening in May 1951.

ABOVE RIGHT: *A manager's meeting at Store No. 8 about 1950. General Merchandise Manager Harry Morrison is standing. Seated to his left are (left to right) George Bartell Jr., P.G. Power, and George Bartell Sr.*

Internal Issues Fester

Yet Bartell's seeming success on the surface only masked the internal issues it faced in the early 1950s. The rise of self-service drugstores was siphoning customers away from Bartell Drugs and making its traditional full-service operation obsolete. At the same time, a surge in the number of drive-in restaurants began to gradually reduce Bartell's soda fountain business. This problem worsened with time, and was accentuated at a few of the fountains by freeloaders who would buy something and hang out for a while, then disappear without paying their checks. Bartell stores were also smaller than some of the newer self-service stores and thus unable to carry enough different types of merchandise to meet the competition.

Finally, all the store managers were registered pharmacists, but they lacked the time and experience to handle the needed changes in their stores' operations and merchandising. This also weighed on Bartell's business, though Bartell Drugs advertised its registered pharmacists as a plus. (However, George Bartell Jr. wasn't a pharmacist, and this became a problem in the early 1950s after the Washington State Legislature passed a law requiring the state's drugstore owners to be registered pharmacists. As a result, he returned to the University of Washington and obtained his pharmacy degree in 1953. Ironically, the law was later struck down.)

Certainly by 1955, the company's problems were glaringly apparent. Wages and expenses were rising, but profits were generally flat. Even when Bartell Drugs enjoyed a good year in the first half of the 1950s, it wasn't enough to get the company back on track. There is some suggestion that the senior Bartell may have

Bartell's Food Operations

Bartell's food operations were one of the biggest parts of its business for many years, representing at least a quarter of its sales during the company's peak years in the 1930s and early 1940s.

George Bartell only reluctantly opened his first soda fountain at his Owl Drugstore in 1902 but added more over the ensuing years as they became more popular. Given their success, he then opened tearooms (restaurants) and a cafeteria in several of his stores. By 1940, Bartell's served more than ten thousand meals a day. Ten years later it had soda fountains in twenty of its twenty-one stores (the exception being its Boren Avenue store) and claimed to have the largest soda fountain business in the Northwest.

Though meals in the early years were prepared in the stores themselves, Bartell's menus expanded to the point where this became impractical. The company had an ice cream plant in its headquarters on Boren Avenue by 1916, but this was just the beginning. By the 1930s, Bartell's was handling most of its food operations out of its food commissary at 1726 Minor Avenue. (Short orders, such as sandwiches, were still made in the drugstores.) Hot food was prepared daily in the commissary's main-floor kitchen and sent to Bartell stores shortly before mealtime. The building also served as the company's food storage center and interview office for all who applied to work at Bartell's fountains.

The commissary's food director prepared daily menus that frequently featured specials. For example, chicken pot pie was the special during Bartell's weeklong sixty-fifth anniversary celebration in 1955. However, the stores offered other meals on a regular basis that were customer favorites. Chili con carne was one. Others included homemade soups made in large pressure cookers and a chipped ham sandwich said to be unique to Bartell's.

A diner could order any number of tasty treats for dessert. One was the Lover's Delight, which featured three kinds of fruit, two kinds of ice cream, and crushed walnuts. But customers weren't limited to what was on the menu. If they wanted their own special dessert, Bartell's would make it if the ingredients were available.

Times changed, and Bartell's soda fountain business began to slowly taper off during the 1950s. This trend accelerated over time, and the commissary closed about 1960. Meals were still prepared in soda fountain and tearoom kitchens, but these, too, gradually disappeared, until Bartell's finally closed its last soda fountain in 1982.

Today, you can buy fresh salads and sandwiches in Bartell's downtown locations and processed food in all its drugstores. There's plenty of packaged candy, crackers, milk, and eggs, and you might even find a frozen pizza. Bartell's 4th Avenue and Madison Street store has a latte stand, and its store at 5th Avenue and Olive Street serves fresh coffee. Soft drinks, energy drinks, and fruit juices are also available at Bartell stores. But it's hardly the same.

FACING PAGE AND ABOVE, LEFT TO RIGHT: *Bartell's University District store dining area, ca. 1948.*

"Bartell soda fountain girls" (and a short-order cook behind them) at the Northgate soda fountain, ca. 1955.

Soda fountain patrons both ignore and stare down the photographer at Bartell's Store No. 23 on Mercer Street in February 1948.

ABOVE: *Bartell triangle store tearoom menu cover and inside page, 1952.*

Bartell's TEA ROOM Menu

Bartell's CELEBRATES 62 YEARS OF PROGRESS WITH SEATTLE

TRIANGLE STORE WESTLAKE PINE 4TH AVE
NORTHGATE STORE

Seattle's Own Drug Stores

BARTELL DRUGS

Steaks and Chops from Our Grill

Tenderoast Steak	
Chicken Fried Steak	
Choice Minute Steak	
Ground Round Steak	
Veal Chops (2)	
Center Cut Pork Chops (2)	

French Fries or Hash Browned Potatoes Served with Above Orders
Order of French Fried Potatoes 20c

Sea Foods

Grilled Salmon or Halibut Steak, French Fries	75c
Fried Oysters, French Fries	75c
Oyster Stew with Buttered Toast	65c

Cocktails and Relishes

Fresh Crab	70c
Celery Hearts	30c
Fruit Salad	20c
Tomato Juice	Small 15c; Large 25c

Eggs and Omelettes

Ham or Bacon and Eggs	75c
Minced Ham Omelette	65c
Eggs Vienna	70c
Spanish Omelette	65c
Plain Omelette	50c
Tomato Omelette	65c
Jelly Omelette	60c
Cheese Omelette	65c
Two Poached Eggs on Toast	45c
Two Eggs Fried, Boiled or Scrambled	45c

Cold Plates

Assorted Cold Meats with Potato Salad and Tomatoes	70c
Cold Roast Beef, Potato Salad	70c
Cold Sliced Chicken with Sliced Tomatoes	80c
Cold Baked Ham with Potato Salad	65c
Cold Kippered Salmon with Potato Salad	70c

Fruits and Juices

Had Your Health Cocktail Today?

Tomato Juice	Small 15c; Large 25c
Grapefruit Juice	Small 15c; Large 25c
Pineapple Juice	Small 15c; Large 30c
V-8 Cocktail	15c
Orange Juice (freshly squeezed), small	15c
Large	30c
Pears	15c	Sliced Orange	20c
Sliced Pineapple	25c	Apple Sauce	10c
Sliced Bananas, cream	30c

Chef's Daily Special

SALADS on Parade

Always in Season — Made to Suit Your Individual Taste

No. 1	PINEAPPLE NUT SALAD — Pineapple — Shredded Lettuce, Mayonnaise Dressing — Chopped Nuts — Roll and Butter	35¢
No. 2	BARTELL'S SPECIAL FRUIT SALAD — Made of Choicest Diced Fruits, on Shredded Lettuce, Chopped Nuts — Buttered Toast	45¢
No. 3	STUFFED TOMATO SALAD — Whole Tomato filled with Chicken Salad, Egg Wedges, on Crisp Lettuce — Toast	55¢
No. 4	AVOCADO SALAD — Sliced Avocado with Fruit Salad 1000 Island Dressing, Buttered Toast	60¢
No. 5	COMBINATION SALAD — Shredded Lettuce, Peas, Sliced Tomatoes, Asparagus Tips and Quartered Hard Boiled Egg; Choice of Dressing — Buttered Toast	60¢
No. 6	TOMATO SURPRISE — Stuffed Tomato with Chicken Salad on Shredded Lettuce, Asparagus Tips, Mayonnaise Dressing — Roll and Butter	65¢
No. 7	COMBINATION SANDWICH AND SALAD — Sliced Turkey Sandwich with Fruit Salad	75¢
No. 8	RUSSIAN SALAD — Chipped Ham, Turkey, Cheese, Celery on Shredded Lettuce, Peas, Tomatoes, Garnish of Hard Boiled Egg, Choice of Dressing, Roll and Butter	80¢
No. 9	DEEP SEA CRAB LOUIE — Deep Sea Crab Meat on Shredded Lettuce, Sliced Tomatoes, Hard Boiled Egg, Potato Salad, French Dressing — Buttered Toast	95¢
No. 10	Our Own Famous Potato Salad Rolls and Butter	25¢

Miscellaneous Salads

Peach and Cottage Cheese on Bed of Lettuce	45c
Pineapple and Cottage Cheese on Bed of Lettuce	45c
Sliced Tomatoes and Lettuce Salad, French Dressing	25c
Chicken Salad on Bed of Lettuce, Sliced Tomatoes	60c
Pear and Cottage Cheese on Bed of Lettuce	45c

resisted some of the changes necessary to turn the company around, but it's not clear if he played a direct role in delaying these changes.

FATHER AND SON

A comment made by George Bartell Sr. in his 1950 KIRO radio interview provides a hint of the dynamics within the company and sheds light on the relationship between father and son. Though George

Bartell Jr. was president of the company, his father referred to him during the interview as "one of the main helpers." The interviewer picked up on this and remarked, "I like that word 'helper,' because you're still the boss. Is that right?" Bartell Sr. demurred, claiming the business was run without a boss.

Likewise, a 1950 *Seattle Times* article about George Bartell Jr. remarked that he was "somewhat following -in his father's footprints." This was a little unfair to the younger Bartell, who would have had to fill some big shoes to match his father's. Still, it's true that he was a much quieter personality, and far more subtle. So it's likely that George Bartell Jr. did not force the issue in making some of the changes to the degree necessary while his father was still alive. His reluctance may have come from deference to his father, or he may simply have not wanted to take the risks required to make big changes to the company unless he felt there was no other choice.

CHANGE IN THE AIR

That's not to say that Bartell Drugs was doing nothing. By 1955, the company was making some changes. One of the more notable ones had come in December 1953, when Bartell's opened its first store across Lake Washington on 104th Avenue NE (now Bellevue Way) in Bellevue. The store was located across the street from Bellevue Square, the Pacific Northwest's first regional shopping center, which had opened eight years earlier. It was a bold move into a brand new city that was just beginning to come into its own (Bellevue had incorporated earlier that year). Significantly, Bartell Drugs billed the new store as a self-service drugstore. And in May 1955, the company opened its second Eastside store, Store No. 6, on S 3rd Street in Renton.

Bartell's was making other changes as well in 1955, particularly with its merchandising. A glance at a Bartell Drugs ad for its sixty-fifth anniversary sale that spring shows the stores selling merchandise that would not have been found at a Bartell drugstore just a few years earlier. Examples include outdoor paint and brushes, garden hoses, and a fountain brush attachment for the garden hose that could be used to clean a car or house. You could even buy a utility box at a Bartell Drugs, good for storing fishing tackle or tools.

TOP: *George Bartell, ca. late 1940s.*

ABOVE: *A photo montage of George Bartell Jr. taken shortly after his return to Bartell Drugs in 1946.*

On the pharmaceutical side, the big new thing at Bartell Drugs in 1955 was nasal spray, good for applying antihistamines (which had only become widely available in the 1940s) to fight colds and allergies. Antihistamines were initially hailed by many as wonder drugs, and some believed they could cure a cold. They couldn't, but they did provide the first dependable relief for some cold and allergy symptoms.

Change was in the air at Bartell Drugs in 1955, but the changes being made were tentative at best. And they weren't really enough. This would become painfully apparent in the next few years, as the company would drastically downsize and close nearly half its stores and its photo lab, and gradually taper off its food operations. There were many in Bartell management who either didn't see what was coming or didn't want to. But that would soon change with the passing of George Bartell Sr.

LEFT ABOVE: *Bartell's original Bellevue store on what is today Bellevue Way, 1950s.*

LEFT BELOW: *A look inside Bartell's first Eastside store, Bellevue, mid-1950s.*

ABOVE: *Bartell's Renton store in the early 1960s.*

CHAPTER 5

Crisis
(1956–1965)

George Bartell Sr. remained active in his company until the end of his life. Known as an ardent sportsman, he had once remarked that the greatest sport of all was the thrill of business. An exuberant, confident man who loved being with other people, Bartell wasn't going to quit on his own, and he didn't.

But as winter edged into spring in March 1956, he fell seriously ill. He was hospitalized for about a week, and died on the afternoon of March 30. After a private funeral and brief period of mourning, the company got back to business.

"Policy At Bartell's Unchanged," reassured a headline to a *Seattle Times* article on April 19, 1956. George Bartell Jr. elaborated: "We are very proud of my father's policies, his desire to treat customers the best way he knew how and to procure for them the right kinds of merchandise at the right prices. ... There is no business I would rather be in today. The Bartell Drug Company is to me a living monument to my father's memory and I hope to be able to continue on the course he so ably set up." Certainly, the company's policies toward customer service did not change with the passing of George Bartell, but many other aspects of the company soon would.

CASH-FLOW WOES

The elder Bartell had recognized the trend toward self-service. And he'd embraced the company's expansion to the Eastside in the mid-1950s, explaining in a 1954 *Seattle Times* interview, "In business there is no such thing as standing still. You have to expand. You get left behind if you think what you did yesterday is good enough for today."

The problem with this approach was its overriding focus on expansion, without addressing the other issues the company faced. By 1956, the company's revenues had been erratic for more than 10

OPPOSITE: *A view of the monorail entrance and Bartell's triangle store, 1963.*

ABOVE: *An article in* The Seattle Times *three weeks after George Bartell's 1956 death reassured readers that the "Policy at Bartell's (is) Unchanged."*

years, with the net result that it was just breaking even. (It was a blessing that George Bartell Sr. had stuck to his policy of incurring as little debt as possible; otherwise, the situation would have been more precarious.) After expanding to the Eastside, Bartell's lacked the capital to make needed updates to its downtown stores. Worse, many of them were now considered too small by the expanding standards of the 1950s and couldn't be updated. Management at many of these stores was an additional problem.

In terms that would become popular years later, Bartell Drugs needed to reorganize and downsize to get back on track. This included closing less-profitable stores and laying off personnel who were unwilling or unable to adjust. Yet it seems that the senior Bartell was not interested in making these changes while he was alive, and George Bartell Jr. did not force the issue. Thus, by the time George Jr. fully assumed responsibility for the company in the spring of 1956, these problems had worsened from festering so long.

REORGANIZING AND DOWNSIZING

Once he settled in, Bartell wasted little time getting started. He felt that one of the most urgent problems was the company's management. This included store managers as well as the upper management team in the company's office. At the same time, he realized that his strength lay more in managing others than in being a kinetic leader like his father. As a result, he sought to bring in talented management, at store and office levels, who could identify the company's problems and contribute their own ideas and experience to solve them. Within a year of his father's passing, he began to assemble a new team.

Early in 1957, Bartell asked for the resignation of P. G. Power, vice president of Bartell Drugs, who had long been considered George Bartell Sr.'s right-hand man. He hired Leonard Ross, an ex-manager from the downtown Seattle Pay'n Save, as the company's general sales manager. Ross had good experience in pharmacy merchandising. He knew what would sell in a drugstore and who to hire to sell it. But he wasn't a pharmacist, while most of Bartell's managers still were. This put Ross at a disadvantage. Though he made some merchandising changes and brought in some good personnel, it wasn't enough to pull the company out of its slump.

TOP: *Bartell's Store No. 9 in Greenwood, 1959. The store was at this location from 1958 until 2013, when it moved next door.*

ABOVE: *George Bartell Jr. and P.G. Power at Bartell's sixty-sixth anniversary dinner, April 1956.*

LEFT: *Bartell's new Burien store, August 1957.*
RIGHT: *Bartell's new White Center store on opening day, December 8, 1959.*

Bartell Drugs also began quietly closing some of its poorly performing stores. The company had closed a few stores in the past, but not with the frequency that it began closing them in the late 1950s. Between September 1957 and the end of 1959, Bartell's closed four stores. This included its store on 2nd Avenue and Pike Street, open for nearly thirty-five years and considered one of Bartell's bigger stores in its heyday. The company's employee count likewise dropped, from more than five hundred employees at the beginning of the 1950s to about four hundred at the decade's end.

These closures were masked by a couple of new stores that opened in areas where Bartell's had not gone before. In 1957, Bartell Drugs moved its Store No. 2 from Seattle to a new building in Burien. It was a handsome building for its day (one suspects George Bartell Jr. supervised its construction, as he had the Bellevue store in 1953), with a diamond pattern decorating its exterior.

Bartell Drugs also opened a new store in White Center late in 1959. Recognizing that parking had been — and still was — a problem at many of its stores (especially the ones downtown), Bartell's publicized that the new store's parking lot was nineteen thousand square feet. Additionally, the store proudly announced that it would sell records, following a trend between the 1950s and the 1970s of drugstores venturing into the music business.

MINORITY SHAREHOLDERS

As the 1950s ended, yet another issue was bubbling beneath the surface. Bartell Drugs had had minority shareholders since its 1910 acquisition of the Raven Drugstore on 2nd Avenue. The Raven Drugstore's purchase was made with Bartell Drug Company stock, creating a group of shareholders with a minority interest in the company. For the next forty or forty-five years, these shareholders were generally a passive presence.

That began to change in the early 1950s. Perhaps realizing that the company's glory days had dissipated, the shareholders became more vocal. In 1958, Stewart Ballinger became a company trustee. Ballinger, a radio-station owner (later active in commercial real estate), was a third-generation Seattleite and well-known in the city. He took a more assertive role in Bartell's affairs than any prior minority shareholder. In part because of his influence, the minority shareholders would become even more outspoken as the company's woes worsened over the next few years.

MORE STORES ARE CLOSED

The 1960s did not get off to a promising start. Late in January 1960 Bartell Drugs closed two long-time stores, including the Aurora Avenue store that had generated such excitement when it opened in 1940. Despite these closures, George Bartell Jr. projected an optimistic front in a *Seattle Times* article that March announcing the company's seventieth anniversary: "As Seattle expands, so we hope to expand the Bartell Drug Company [by] putting in more modern stores," adding that the company planned further expansion that spring. In June, the company moved its Ballard store from its Market Street location to a newer building on 22nd Avenue NW. In the sense that this was a bigger store, Bartell's did expand. But this was a move, not an additional new store.

There were more closures in 1961. In a two-month period between August and October, the company closed six of its downtown stores. These closings included its store at the entrance to

G. Henbart Company

The G. Henbart Company is a commercial real estate investment company, formed in 1922 by George Bartell Sr. The name G. Henbart represents Bartell's first initial, and a combination of his middle and last names. Over the years, the Henbart Company has purchased property that it subsequently leased to Bartell Drugs for its stores. However, the company has bought property for other purposes. For example, Henbart purchased several lots in Meadowdale in the mid-1930s, and George Bartell subsequently built his rural retreat on two of these lots.

Along with other real estate companies, Henbart suffered when land prices declined during the Depression. At the same time, Bartell Drugs prospered. As a result, Bartell combined Henbart with the Bartell Drug Company in 1940, with Henbart becoming the parent company and Bartell Drugs a wholly owned subsidiary. In an ironic twist, it turned out to be good timing: When Bartell Drugs struggled financially between the 1940s and mid-1960s, Henbart provided loans to the company to help it meet its cash flow needs.

George Bartell Jr. developed an interest in design and construction as a young man, and did much of the layout work for new and remodeled Bartell drugstores for nearly his entire career. Henbart provided Bartell with an opportunity to develop this interest further, and he took advantage of it. He managed the Henbart Company in the early 1960s, and though he subsequently returned to a more active role at Bartell Drugs, his interest in property development remained. He soon took on a project that he would be especially proud of, and one that Jean Bartell Barber has described as his life dream.

Henbart had purchased nine lots along the western shore of Lake Union in 1949, and Bartell saw the potential in developing this property. In 1969, he designed a seven-story office building for the site at 1700 Westlake Avenue N, and bought another lot for a parking structure just south of the existing property. Building permits were issued later that year, and the $3.25 million project took nearly two years to complete. The Lake Union Building opened in September 1971. A marina (presently known as the Lake Union Building Marina) followed in 1980.

The relationship between Henbart and Bartell Drugs was restructured in 1986, and Henbart became a division of Bartell Drugs. In 2008 Henbart added a president, Mark Craig, and a separate board of directors to more actively manage its real estate portfolio. In 2013, Bartell Drugs and Henbart became wholly owned subsidiaries of a new parent company, B. Alliance Holdings, Inc.

Today, Henbart develops, owns, and manages commercial real estate properties in King and Snohomish counties. Like Bartell's, Henbart concentrates its efforts in the Puget Sound region and reinvests locally.

A sketch of a proposal for the Lake Union Building, ca. 1969.

TOP: *George Bartell Jr. and Fred Damlos at the opening of the new Bellevue store, 1962.*

ABOVE: *The Bartell family in 1964. Robert, Betty, and Jean Bartell are in front; George Bartell Jr. and George D. Bartell stand behind.*

Pike Place Market, open since 1908. At the end of October 1961, Bartell Drugs had twelve stores in operation, down from a peak of twenty-three just five years earlier. Bartell's also sold its Minor Avenue property — headquarters of its food operations — to Diamond Parking in 1961. And in September of that year, George Bartell Jr. asked for the resignation of his sales manager, Leonard Ross.

ENTER FRED DAMLOS

In October 1961, Fred Damlos was hired as general manager. Damlos, the former director of merchandising for Rexall Drugs in Los Angeles, seemed a good fit for the job. A bright and urbane man with considerable retail merchandising experience, he had a number of ideas for the company and is said to have told Bartell that under his guidance, Bartell Drugs would make a profit within three years.

There was an uptick in 1962. Bartell's relocated its Bellevue store into a newer and larger building behind its old store on Bellevue Way. This store was far more geared toward self-service, and at nearly twelve thousand square feet, was one of Bartell's bigger stores. After a slow start, the store became one of the company's more successful Eastside drugstores, and one of its more enduring, remaining at this location for nearly fifty years.

The 1962 Seattle World's Fair generated tremendous excitement in the city and more revenue from increased tourist traffic. Bartell Drugs enjoyed a similar surge in business, especially at its downtown triangle store, which was fortuitously located next to the southern terminus of the new monorail that was built for the fair. Given the improved performance, Damlos was promoted to company president in June 1963 and Bartell became the chairman of the board.

Then sales dropped. One of the biggest problems was that the company wasn't offering many bargains to bring in customers, who might then make other purchases. However, there was one exception, and it got a lot of press in the Seattle papers: Early in 1963, Bartell's reduced all of its prescription prices 10 percent to its customers over age 60. Bartell Drugs was the first drugstore to do this in Seattle, following the lead of some East Coast drugstores that were offering similar discounts to combat competition from the discount drugstores. Damlos, in announcing the senior citizen discount, candidly admitted in an interview with the *Seattle Post-Intelligencer* that it was being done as a "trade stimulant." The program was quite successful and brought new customers and more business to Bartell's, but by itself, it was not enough to cure the company's ills.

Bartell Drugs found itself caught in a competitive whipsaw, with large discount stores, such as the House of Values, Gov-Mart Bazaar, and drugstore operator Pay'n Save, all providing stiff competition. Pay'n Save, a pharmacy chain opened in Seattle in 1947 by Monte Lafayette Bean, had become extremely successful by the early 1960s and was Bartell's toughest competitor. It attracted customers with plenty of merchandise at low prices in large, modern, attractive stores. At that time, Bartell Drugs offered neither in most of its stores.

More Management Changes

Early in 1964, Bartell's board of directors directed Damlos to talk to an outside management firm about finding other talent to help manage the company. What exactly happened afterward is unclear, other than that outside talent was found and lengthy negotiations ensued. As a result of these negotiations, Bartell obtained Damlos's resignation and again became president of the company. At the same time, Bartell Drugs entered into an eighteen-month revocable contract with two men, George Kanrich and Robert Thornberg, to serve as the company's administrative vice president and operations manager, respectively. Damlos's resignation was effective September 1, 1964, and Kanrich and Thornberg took their new positions the same day.

In August 1963 Bartell Drugs held a drawing for a free 1963 Rambler to celebrate its Bellevue store opening. Shown are the happy winners.

The Triangle Store and the World's Fair

The 1962 Seattle World's Fair dazzled Seattle between April and October. As part of the fair, a monorail was built that stretched from near the Space Needle on the fairgrounds southeast along 5th Avenue to its southern terminus on Pine Street. Everyone wanted to ride it. And as it turned out, the monorail's southern end was about 20 feet from Bartell's triangle store at 4th Avenue and Pine Street. There could not have been a better spot for the store.

The triangle-shaped store tapered to a narrow blunted point on its south end. It had three floors. The basement offered sundries and seasonal merchandise, including World's Fair souvenirs. The main floor had the pharmacy and some over-the-counter drugs, a soda fountain, cosmetics, and other merchandise. The top floor offered a nice restaurant known as the tearoom.

In 1962, Sanford Barnes was manager of the triangle store. He knew a prime opportunity when he saw one. "This is going to be fantastic," he told Gordon O'Reilly when he hired him to work in the store in 1961. And it was. Though O'Reilly went on to have a successful 42-year career with Bartell Drugs, he described the fair's six months as "probably the single greatest experience … did I ever learn a lot about the retail business." Added Val Storrs, who started work at the store in the middle of the fair's run, "Every few minutes, there was something new happening."

Celebrities and public figures were often in the store. Comedian George Burns stopped by. So did Elvis Presley, in town to film his latest movie, *It Happened at the World's Fair*. O'Reilly, working in the basement, missed him, but recalled other employees dashing down to tell him Elvis had just left

the building. He did meet William F. Buckley Jr., a conservative writer and commentator, who stopped by several times. Comedian Charlie Callas also visited the store.

Barnes remembered the more regular folks who came. Many had come from all over the country; a few had come from foreign countries. "I used to go down and talk with all the people from different parts of the world," he said. "I couldn't speak [their language] but I could tell them how to get food — and that restaurant upstairs [the tearoom] was really good!"

Ever the salesman, Barnes didn't limit himself to food. Early on, he visited the fair and priced some of the souvenirs — plates, mugs, tumblers, and spoons, all with the World's Fair insignia. He bought large quantities of them from a friendly vendor, and then turned around and sold them at the store for slightly less than the fair's prices. Laughed Storrs fifty years later, "If you'd seen our stock room stocked with all those souvenirs, you'd have thought we were nuts. And some people did. But they sold!"

You didn't even have to go in the store if you wanted one. Bartell's opened a window on the side of the building facing the monorail that was staffed during the day with a clerk selling them, as well as cigarettes, candy, and film.

Seattle World's Fair pennant.

This did not solve the problem. Sales continued to stagnate. Advertising was another issue, since there were few significant bargains being offered to attract customers. The company was focusing more on profits and less on sales, contrary to what it had done in the past. And in some instances, the mix of merchandise being sold — for example, Bartell Drugs stocked curtain rods in large quantities for a time — was wrong for a drugstore.

STRIKE!

In the mid-1930s George Bartell Sr. had invited a pharmacist-clerk union to organize in his stores, because he felt it would be good for his employees. While this was a remarkably progressive approach for any company owner, it created a new set of issues for Bartell Drugs. By the 1960s, nearly all the company's employees were members of Local 330 of the Pharmacists and Retail Drug Store Employees Union, which most of them were required to join by the terms of Bartell's contract with the union.

As 1964 wound down, the union struck. The strike centered on a wage dispute between the union and management, and it affected more than three hundred drugstores in King and South Snohomish counties. However, Bartell's upper management had not alerted its store managers to the pending strike, and more than a few of them had no idea what was coming.

On Thursday morning, December 3, they opened their stores as usual. Then they began wondering why their employees weren't showing up. Soon enough, they began arriving — as picketers. Managers found themselves hiring customers who came in off the street to work as clerks.

RETAIL DRUG
AGREEMENT

OCTOBER 1, 1968 TO
SEPTEMBER 30, 1970

BETWEEN

PHARMACISTS AND RETAIL DRUG STORE
EMPLOYEES UNION

LOCAL NO. 330, R.C.I.A., AFL-CIO
2819 1ST AVE., SEATTLE, WASHINGTON 98121

AND

THE RETAIL DRUG STORE OPERATORS

REPRESENTED BY THE

SEATTLE-KING COUNTY
PHARMACEUTICAL SOCIETY

AND THE

GREATER SEATTLE
RETAIL DRUG ASSOCIATION

Booklet detailing contract terms between members of the Seattle-King County Pharmaceutical Society and the Greater Seattle Retail Drug Association (which included Bartell Drugs) and the Pharmacists and Retail Drugstore Employees Union, 1968-1970.

(This actually worked to a surprising degree.) Of course, hiring registered pharmacists was not that simple. Replacement pharmacists had to be brought in from as far away as Idaho. The strike lasted thirteen days, ending in time for the stores to salvage what was left of the Christmas shopping season. But it was a dismal end to a difficult year.

AN UNHAPPY NEW YEAR

Bartell Drugs got off to an equally cheerless start in 1965. Nothing seemed to be working. The store managers were demoralized. Some were eyeing opportunities with other companies. One day Bartell held a meeting with his store managers to discuss what was happening and to hear their thoughts about the direction being taken by Kanrich and Thornberg. Sanford Barnes, manager of the triangle store, offered his assessment: "Mr. Bartell, I hear you have a real nice house in Magnolia. When you have to sell it, let me know. I'd like to buy it, because this program isn't going to work."

Bartell was shocked. He shouldn't have been — Barnes was not a shrinking violet. Besides, other store managers were telling him the same thing. It didn't take him long to reach the same conclusion.

STORRS AND O'REILLY TAKE CHARGE

In February 1965, Bartell terminated the company's contract with Kanrich and Thornberg. He promoted Bellevue store manager Val Storrs to operations manager and Ballard store manager Gordon O'Reilly to merchandise manager. Storrs had started as a clerk at Bartell's triangle store in 1962. Though he had no prior pharmaceutical experience, he had a natural talent for retail and understood how to bring in customers, as well as how to hire quality talent. Within eight months of being hired, he was managing Bartell's Queen Anne store. O'Reilly likewise had no pharmaceutical experience before starting as a clerk in 1961 (also at the triangle store). However, he demonstrated a keen talent for merchandising and moved up quickly in the ranks. By the beginning of 1965 he was managing Bartell's Ballard store.

Both men not only understood the business well, they also had keen intuitive skills for how to get the company moving forward again. Bartell recognized these skills and gave them free rein to

TOP: *J. L. Terrill, regional manager for the pharmaceutical company Squibb, presents pharmacist Lionel Gilmore (left) and George Bartell Jr. (right) with a plaque commemorating Bartell Drugs filling eight million prescriptions since 1890, March 1962.*

BELOW: *Bartell pharmacist Lionel Gilmour beams as he reads about Bartell's new Senior Citizens Prescription Plan in* The Seattle Times, *1963.*

make changes. It was precisely what the company needed, but in 1965 this wasn't yet obvious.

EXIT MINORITY SHAREHOLDERS

The minority shareholders were furious with these developments and with Bartell's more assertive management of the company. To add fuel to their fire, they'd seen the book value of their company shares fall by more than half since George Bartell Sr.'s death nine years earlier. They threatened to force Bartell Drugs into receivership because of alleged mismanagement and corporate abuse in several areas — leases of its properties, inventory control, personnel, and accounting, to name a few.

They also alleged that Bartell's interest with its then-parent company, G. Henbart Company, created a conflict of interest. The Henbart Company was, and remains, a commercial real estate company that was formed by George Bartell Sr. in 1922. George Bartell Jr. had turned his attention to managing this company during the turbulent years in the early 1960s when he was not running Bartell Drugs. Managing a real estate company was something of a natural for Bartell given his interest in property development, but it gave the minority shareholders another arrow in their quiver.

They decided they wanted out, and demanded that Bartell purchase their shares of company stock. He did, paying considerably less than full book value. The buyout was completed in October 1965.

This ended the last of the problems that had plagued Bartell Drugs for so long. No one knew it yet, just as no one had known twenty-five years earlier that the company was at a peak. But 1965 was the turning point, and over the next few years the company slowly — almost imperceptibly at first — began the trek back toward stability and growth.

SPRINGBOARD TO SUCCESS

As far back as the company's seventy-second anniversary dinner in March 1962, George Bartell Jr. had outlined plans for modernizing its twelve existing stores. Bartell Drugs took the first step toward implementing this plan late in 1964 when it renovated its store on the corner of NE 45th Street and University Way NE. "This remodeling is actually the first of a series of projects that will be carried

P. G. Power

Percival George Power (known as P. G. Power) was born in Manitoba in 1894 and moved to Seattle in 1900. In 1916, he served with more than a thousand other Washington State guardsmen in a camp in the border town of Calexico, California, where the guard had been sent in response to attacks on Americans by Mexican revolutionary Pancho Villa. He later served in the Army Medical Corps during World War I.

The war ended in November 1918 and Power was discharged. He was so broke that he had no clothes other than his Army pharmacist's uniform. But this uniform seems to have served him well, because early in 1919, he went to work for Bartell Drugs. He was initially in charge of the prescription department at the Bartell store on 1st Avenue and Pike Street, at the entrance to Pike Place Market.

Power quickly impressed George Bartell, and after a few years was promoted to manager of the Pike Place Market store. Soon after, he was also named manager of the store at 2nd Avenue and Union Street and later managed the Bartell store at 2nd Avenue and Pike Street. The Pike Street stores were two of the company's bigger and more important stores. Managing these stores in addition to his other duties gave Power considerable clout.

He rose through the ranks to become advertising manager, sales manager, and, by 1935, general manager.

P.G. Power, 1950.

By 1950, he had been vice president of Bartell Drugs for a number of years, in charge of company operations. George Bartell Jr. acknowledges in his memoir that Power was considered to be "my father's right-hand man," even though Bartell Jr. was president of the company for some of those years.

However, the relationship between George Bartell Jr. and Power was considerably cooler. One can sense it just by looking at the body language of the two men in a picture of them seated together at the company dinner in April 1956, a few weeks after George Bartell Sr.'s death. The chill is underscored by Bartell Jr.'s polite but curt mention of Power in his memoir.

Power resigned from Bartell Drugs in March 1957, but this was for the sake of appearances; Bartell had asked him to leave. But his resignation would likely have soon followed in any event. His health had begun to fail about a year earlier, and he died at his home in Seattle's Broadview neighborhood in 1958.

In addition to his duties at Bartell Drugs, Power served as the president of the Seattle Chamber of Commerce Retail Trade Bureau for several years during the 1950s. He also served as president of the Seattle Shopping News, a shopping paper owned by its advertisers (which included Bartell Drugs) that operated for about half a century between the 1920s and the 1970s.

out in the future," explained Bartell in an interview with *The Seattle Times* that December.

This is where Storrs and O'Reilly would come in. Over the next ten or so years, they would take the lead in modernizing Bartell's stores and its overall business in a process that the company would call "self-modernization." It would prove to be a springboard to success as Bartell Drugs moved into the final decades of the twentieth century.

MENU

CHAPTER 6

Self-Modernization
(1966-1979)

T he Bartell Drug Company's recent lack of success with hiring outside managers prompted George Bartell Jr. to address as many of the company's problems as he could from within. There also was a practical reason for this approach — a shortage of extra capital to bring in outside assistance. Thus, self-modernization meant Bartell Drugs would be updating the company's stores and internal operations on its own, without bringing in outside contractors or managers to do the job.

Storrs and O'Reilly found themselves with a big task ahead in remodeling the stores. Though Bartell's had some modern stores in the 1960s (such as its new one in Bellevue), more of them were outdated. Shoppers bypassed Bartell stores and patronized competitors' drugstores, especially Pay'n Save. Storrs and O'Reilly's goal was to change that.

OPPOSITE: *Cover of Bartell Drugs breakfast menu, 1969.*

ABOVE RIGHT: *A relaxed George Bartell Jr. confidently greets a new decade in 1970.*

CARPENTRY WORK

In some ways emulating the Pay'n Save model of well-stocked, good-looking stores, the two men proceeded. Bartell gave them plenty of leeway, though he kept a tight rein on the purse strings. On many days Storrs and O'Reilly worked their regular office jobs until 5 p.m., then headed to the warehouse for an evening of carpentry work. With warehouse manager Nels Muir, the men made fixtures (primarily shelves but also cashier stands) for Bartell's stores. On other nights, they worked well into the night installing the fixtures in the stores. Not only was this extra effort cost-effective, but it was a morale booster for all Bartell employees — not just for the management team, who eventually began to see the fruits of their labor, but for lower-level employees too, who were impressed that upper management spent their nights working to improve the company's stores.

Storrs and O'Reilly also felt that it made sense to make the stores look as uniform as they could. "Our aim was to make our stores to the point that you could go in with a blindfold, take it off, and say 'Oh, this is a Bartell's store,'" O'Reilly explained. At first this wasn't entirely possible, because the stores differed so widely in size. But in the ensuing years, Bartell Drugs closed or moved its smaller stores to bigger buildings, making it possible to provide a more uniform look.

Self-modernization of all the Bartell stores lasted well into the 1970s. By the late 1970s, the stores began to resemble what we know today, with well-lit, wide aisles and low shelves, not only to enable customers to easily reach merchandise but also to let them see all over the stores.

MERCHANDISING CHANGES

As merchandise manager, O'Reilly made changes to both how the company ordered and handled its merchandise and how Bartell Drugs advertised its products. Both O'Reilly and Storrs felt that the company's advertising was being mishandled. Bartell's prices weren't competitive, and discounts needed to be advertised more aggressively to bring in customers.

O'Reilly felt the problem went further than that. He believed that *what* was advertised also had to change. His idea was to bring in customers for items they'd really need, not just what they might want. "Vitamin C was a prime example," he elaborated. "It went on from there. We'd find something at a low price in volume, and sell it with low markup." And if Bartell's could beat Pay'n Save's prices, so much the better.

O'Reilly also changed how the company handled its inventory and supplied its stores. Twenty years after the end of World War II, Bartell Drugs was still stocking its warehouse with sundry items (such as cosmetics) much as it had during the war, with large quantities of inventory stockpiled to supply its stores as needed. Bartell stores ordered many of these sundries from the company's warehouse, not from a supplier.

Moving Forward

In 1890, my father, George H. Bartell, Sr., founded The Bartell Drug Company. Until his death in 1956, he exercised great influence over the growth and development of our group of stores. When I became president of the Company in 1939, there were certain fundamental policies that he and I agreed should never be changed so long as either of us were responsible for management.

• • •

Foremost among these policies was that Bartell Drug Stores must always maintain the highest standards of integrity . . . that our sales people be sincerely warm and friendly . . . that only quality merchandise be carried . . . that our prices be truly competitive . . . that our prescription departments maintain the highest standards, deserving the complete trust of both physician and customer . . . that our stores be conveniently located, amply stocked, clean and attractive . . . that we are primarily *drug stores* and as such must carry merchandise that people desire and expect to find in good *drug stores*.

• • •

I mention the past only because that past is indelibly linked with Bartell's future. The policies above will continue to be the foundation upon which we will grow and give constantly improved service to you in the Greater Seattle area.

• • •

However, we need to look forward and to move forward. Because of population shifts, certain of our locations are not as convenient as they once were. Because of the need for an increased variety of some lines of merchandise, certain of our stores are inadequate in size. For these two reasons we will close several of our older stores and open new ones as proper locations are determined. The remaining stores will be put to the acid test

of the policies outlined in this message. This will mean considerable remodeling in some instances. It will mean the newest, most modern service features in all instances.

• • •

Yet, we will remain *drug stores* — for that is what you want us to be. Convenience items, yes, but fundamentally you will find in Bartell's those items *you* want to find in drug stores.

• • •

You will always know, when you bring a prescription to Bartell's, that your doctor's instructions will be followed exactly. Our pharmacists' skill is assured — their standards are the highest — by years of exhaustive study. They are aware of — and by constant study and research keep abreast of — the rapid advances in pharmacology, advances that occur almost daily. Because of this, they are able to dispense the thousands of drugs and medicinals, both old and new, commonly or rarely used, that constitute modern medicine. Your physician trusts them implicitly to do this precisely, efficiently, safely. You too, can put your trust in them.

• • •

We are not interested in selling inferior merchandise cheaper — we are only interested in providing you with quality merchandise at very competitive prices.

• • •

Bartells have been *your* drug stores for many, many years. As we move forward with better stores, more conveniently located, we hope to merit your continuing confidence for many years to come. We will do our utmost to deserve it.

G. H. Bartell, Jr.
President, Bartell Drug Stores

The problem with this approach was that some products didn't sell as well or as fast as others and languished in the warehouse for several years. By the time it was needed, a product might be outdated or even obsolete. Other products, such as lipstick, eventually deteriorated and were worthless after a few years. "We cut that out quick," recalled O'Reilly. He instead turned the warehouse into a cross-dock distribution center for primarily advertised goods, and Bartell stores began ordering their sundries directly from a supplier. When this merchandise arrived at the warehouse, it was promptly forwarded to the store that had ordered it.

New Accounting, New Personnel

One of the first things that Storrs tackled was the store's accounting system. The company calculated its profits based on a system set up some years earlier for tax-saving purposes. Under this system, the value of the inventory was written off and expensed as its value depreciated over time. Inventory two years old had no value left on the company's books; therefore, the cost of these goods sold as reflected on Bartell's financial statement had no relation to what the company had actually paid for the merchandise. "It was impossible to tell if we were making money or not," Storrs explained. He worked with Bob Rutherford, Bartell's CPA, to change this system to bring better accuracy to the company books.

An even bigger challenge Storrs faced was updating the pharmacy staff. By the 1960s, many of Bartell's pharmacists were older and set in their ways. Productivity was an issue. But even productive managers, who were also pharmacists, lacked the time and experience to handle the changes that were needed in operations and merchandising. Bartell's would have to bring in new management, but this was a problem at first. Its once-sterling reputation had declined, and talented pharmacists were going elsewhere. In a few cases, Storrs had to hire candidates he wasn't sure of just to fill the positions.

"But little by little we got through it. It took a few years," he said. Late in the 1960s, he also implemented a management-training program to school employees that the company felt had management potential. As time went on, he gradually was able to hire and train younger, more astute pharmacists. His timing couldn't have been better. Later in the 1970s, when pharmacists began to play a more direct role in their customers' health care as part of the rise in clinical pharmacy, Bartell Drugs had a knowledgeable, motivated staff on hand to help.

OPPOSITE: *An undated Bartell publication, likely from the 1960s, explained how Bartell's was moving forward with what later became known as "self-modernization."*

RIGHT: *A Bartell ad in* The Seattle Times *featured a 44 cent sale on April 26, 1966.*

MISSTEP IN EDMONDS

In 1966, Bartell Drugs opened a store in Edmonds. The company had been looking for a suitable location in the area for some time, thinking that it would be a good place for a new store. When an opportunity came up near the ferry terminal, Bartell's took it. (At the same time it closed its Burien store, leaving its store count at twelve.) The new store was in Snohomish County, the company's first store outside of King County, though this was only coincidental.

The store was part of a new $2 million shopping center named Parker Plaza. It was an attractive little shopping center, consisting of about five stores that were "anchored" by a Safeway. (An anchor store is typically a larger store that is considered the major store in a shopping center or mall.) Bartell did much of the layout work for the store interior, while Storrs, O'Reilly, and Nels Muir built and installed many of the store fixtures. All was ready for Parker Plaza's grand opening on October 26, 1966.

At first, the store looked as if it would do well. Then it became apparent that it would not. The problem was a lack of customers. The new store was only two or three blocks from the Edmonds ferry dock, but most of the city was farther east. Customers had to make an effort to drive to Bartell Drugs when other drugstores were closer. Worse, traffic to the dock backed up during busy hours, making access to the store difficult.

There were other problems. The store was less than a quarter mile from Puget Sound. When the tide came in, water backed up under the parking lot's storm grate and flooded part of the plaza's parking lot. Within a few years, mildew began coming up through the store's floor. To make matters worse, the roof leaked. After four years, Bartell Drugs closed the store.

The company learned some good lessons from the experience, and it was more careful in selecting store locations afterward. But it did not have a positive impact on the already risk-averse George Bartell Jr. He became more reluctant to take on any substantial expansion for the next few years. Instead, the focus remained on self-modernization, which provided a solid foundation for the company when it was ready to expand later in the 1970s.

George Bartell Jr.'s children were teenagers during these years. They were becoming old enough to consider summer jobs and other part-time work, as well as think about what careers they might be interested in as they got older. All of them would work for Bartell Drugs, but their career paths would not be similar.

GEORGE D. BARTELL

George D. Bartell had taken inventory for a couple of Bartell stores in his early teens, and he had once washed Bartell's Queen Anne store. But he hadn't thought much about working for the company as he was growing up, and his father hadn't said much to him about it, either. Instead, it was Sanford Barnes who urged him to come to work at the triangle store in the summer of 1968, when he was 16.

"I started in the basement, mostly doing stock work and cashiering. I was a horrible cashier to start out, introverted, looking down more than looking customers in the eye," Bartell recalled. Barnes's recollection of Bartell's early days was more diplomatic. "[He] was a real smart young man, but he had to be trained, and his father didn't train him any," Barnes explained in a 1997 interview. Instead Barnes provided the training, showing Bartell how to buy and sell merchandise, providing advice on customer relations, and often reminding him that it was the customer who was the boss.

86 The Seattle Times   Sunday, October 23, 1966

EDMONDS PARKER PLAZA GRAND OPENING SCHEDULED WEDNESDAY

Edmonds Parker Plaza Opening Is Set

The $2 million Edmonds Parker Plaza will have its grand opening Wednesday.

Businesses opening will be a 21,500 square foot Safeway store, an 8,000 square foot Bartell Drug Store, the Highlander Center Maytag Coin-Op and a 3,000 square foot self-service Washington State liquor store.

A Sprouse-Reitz variety store containing 7,800 square feet will open November 2.

Covered walkways with planting areas will connect the stores. Parking for more than 200 automobiles will be provided.

The H. A. Parker Co. is the developer. Principals are Parker, Realtor and investor; Thomas E. Dunstan, architect, and Raymond C. Brumbach, attorney and president of Security Savings and Loan Association. Financing was arranged by Tom Healy of Sparkman and McLean.

The same developers will open a similar center in Port Townsend in December. Another center is planned to open in Mountlake Terrace late next year.

Hall and Dykman, Everett architectural firm, designed the Safeway store. William Olson, Bellevue, designed the other area.

Dunstan is in charge of construction supervision and leasing.

A Seattle Times article on October 23, 1966, announced the opening of Parker Plaza in Edmonds, and with it Bartell's first store outside of King County.

GORDON O'REILLY

LEFT: *Gordon O' Reilly, ca. 1965.*
RIGHT: *Gordon O'Reilly at Bartell headquarters, 1990.*

Gordon O'Reilly was born in 1937 in Salem, Oregon, but grew up in the tiny town of Scio (about twelve miles northeast of Albany). He enlisted in the Navy the day after graduating from high school and spent the next four years in a naval air transport squadron, traveling to many parts of the world. It was an eye-opening experience for O'Reilly, who had lived a sheltered life growing up in small-town Oregon. By 1957, he was stationed at Sand Point Naval Air Station in Seattle and began taking night courses at the University of Washington. By the time he was discharged, he'd decided he liked Seattle, where he'd by then met his future wife, Laverne, who lived in the city. He got married, continued his studies at the UW, and earned a business degree in 1961.

O'Reilly had worked his way through college, but none of his jobs were related to pharmacy. He hadn't taken any pharmacy classes at the UW, and he wasn't planning on a career in pharmacy. But he was intrigued by a Bartell's ad for management trainees that ran in the UW paper about the time he graduated, and applied for a position. Although he was competing against twenty others for one position, he was the candidate selected.

O'Reilly started with Bartell Drugs in September 1961, working as a clerk in the triangle store under Sanford Barnes. He rose quickly through several assistant manager positions, and by late 1964 was managing Bartell's Ballard store. In 1965 he became the company's merchandise manager, and, along with Val Storrs, helped revitalize Bartell Drugs. He became vice president of merchandising in 1982, and was promoted to senior vice president in 2001. As Bartell Drugs grew during the 1980s and 1990s, O'Reilly supervised merchandise purchases to make sure that stores were stocked properly, and he also supervised the company's advertising and warehouse operations.

He felt that his greatest accomplishment was helping bring the company out of its slump during the 1960s. One of his greatest challenges came at the same time, when he trained new store managers to order the right merchandise and to deal with supplier salesmen, because the pharmacist managers who had previously run the stores hadn't been able to properly handle merchandising issues. He also found the implementation of a point-of-sale scanning system in Bartell's stores during the 1990s to be a challenge but well worth the effort once it was fully implemented.

O'Reilly retired in 2003, and made a couple of observations looking back. "The pharmacy business has grown," he said. "There are more drugs available, and people are living longer and need more drugs. ... But people demand more than they used to. Bartell's biggest advantage is that it has personal service. It can't be overestimated."

He added, "I made a career decision when I was very young that could have gone any number of ways. I'm glad I did what I did and that Bartell's is what it is now and not what it was then [1961]. I'd like to think that Val Storrs and I played a role in that."

LEFT: *George, Jean, and Robert Bartell, ca. 1975.*

FACING PAGE, FROM LEFT: *Bartell's West Seattle store before self-modernization, mid-1970s; Bartell's West Seattle store after self-modernization, late 1970s.*

Bartell soon learned that the company's union contract required that he join the union. "Frankly, I did not want to," he said. "It seemed an imposition to be forced to join an organization that might call me to go on strike against my family business. I did not know what to do." How the problem was solved remains a mystery (though Barnes is suspected of having played a role), but he never joined.

JEAN BARTELL

Jean Bartell gave even less thought to working for Bartell Drugs as she was growing up, later explaining, "People forget [now], but growing up in the '50s and '60s, women weren't supposed to have careers. People didn't talk to girls about that." But she did some inventory work in high school and was curious to learn more about the company. She graduated from Queen Anne High School in 1971, and worked that summer as a retail clerk in the basement of the triangle store. She excelled in cashiering and enjoyed working with the store's customers. She also did some relief work in the cosmetics department, an experience she later laughed about, admitting she then knew little about cosmetics.

However, Jean Bartell's early career years followed a different path than her older brother's. After that summer in 1971, she did not work for Bartell Drugs again for more than twenty years. (She did work part time as a bookkeeper for the Henbart Company during her college years, perhaps a better fit given her aptitude for math.) After graduating magna cum laude from the University of Washington in 1975 with a degree in business administration, she worked for Seafirst as a loan officer in its correspondent banking department for three and a half years. In 1979, she left Seattle to pursue an MBA at The Wharton School of the University of Pennsylvania in Philadelphia.

ROBERT BARTELL

Like his siblings, Bob Bartell did some inventory work for Bartell Drugs as a teenager and also worked summers as a cashier at the triangle store under Sanford Barnes. After graduating from college, he went his own way, as his sister did. He later returned to Bartell Drugs in 1989 and 1990, but decided that the company was not a good fit for him. In 1999, he asked the company and his family to buy out his ownership interest in Bartell Drugs.

ELECTRONIC ORDER TRANSMISSION

In 1973, Bartell Drugs began working with a new supplier, Northwestern Drug. Then based in Tacoma, Northwestern Drug offered lower wholesale costs on strong-selling beauty aids and over-the-counter drugs, and gave its customers access to

manufacturer specials if it still had stock from the special purchase. But what was most significant about Northwestern Drug was its electronic order system. "It was a godsend," said Val Storrs. "It changed our whole method of merchandising and ordering."

In the years before 1973, a supplier's salesman called on Bartell stores once a week and simply wrote on a pad what he thought the store needed. The store manager himself typically had little input. And there was no organized system to track the sale of merchandise in Bartell stores or even to identify where merchandise was placed. If an item ran low or ran out, store employees didn't always know about it until a customer asked for the item. If it wasn't there, the result was not only a lost sale but possibly a lost customer.

Electronic order transmission, which preceded barcodes and scanners, changed all that. Store products were now shelf-tagged with an individual order number for each product. With the use of a handheld ordering device, an employee could simply go through a store and determine what products were low and needed to be replenished. The employee typed the order number for a particular product into the device, put in the quantity needed to replenish that product, and moved on. Once the order was complete, the employee transmitted it over the telephone to Northwestern Drug.

Electronic order transmission made it necessary to assign products specific places on store shelves, something Bartell Drugs

had not done before. As a result, Storrs and O'Reilly developed a merchandising guide suggesting how and where merchandise should be placed, making it easier to find. This was beneficial for Bartell's employees as well as its customers.

George D. Bartell attended Maine's Bowdoin College between 1969 and 1973, returning home in the summers and Christmas holidays to work in the triangle store, and later doing relief work in other Bartell stores. When he graduated in 1973, he returned to Seattle and coordinated the implementation of the new ordering system with all the company's stores, visiting each one weekly and transmitting its order. Once the new system was firmly established, ordering merchandise was turned over to the store employees.

Now the stores could write their own orders. As Storrs pointed out, this was indeed a godsend for several reasons. The most obvious was that the individual store managers and employees knew what sold well at their store and what did not. A wholesaler's salesman was more likely to place a generic order and order the same products for all Bartell stores, without regard to whether the product actually sold at a particular store. And there was always a possibility that the salesman would be motivated to order superfluous supplies for his employer's own profit. Now the store employees could simply order merchandise over the telephone. This allowed individual store managers to customize the product

VAL STORRS

Val Storrs was born in 1931 in American Fork, Utah, and grew up there. After graduating from high school, he spent five years loading blast furnaces at Geneva Steel, then the town's principal employer. He and his older brother subsequently opened a grocery store in American Fork, and Storrs was there for eight years. "It was my introduction to retailing, and I really enjoyed it," he recalled. But he and his brother didn't always agree on things, and Storrs eventually decided to leave. He and his wife, Gertrud, visited Seattle, and decided to move there. After a brief stint at an import-export business, he started at Bartell Drugs as a clerk in its triangle store in July 1962, working under Sanford Barnes.

Though Storrs had no pharmacy experience, he had retail experience and strong views on customer service that served him well as he rose through the ranks. And he rose quickly — by early 1963, he was managing Bartell's Queen Anne store. In 1965 he became company operations manager, and, along with Gordon O'Reilly, helped turn Bartell Drugs back into a thriving company. He became vice president of operations in 1975 and senior vice president in 1980. He took the lead in creating Bartell's human resources department in the mid-1970s and supervised the department for a number of years. Later, he helped acquire new store locations and negotiated the leases necessary for these stores. He also negotiated with the company's union in its periodic contract talks with Bartell Drugs.

Storrs said he felt that his greatest accomplishment was contributing to the successful growth of Bartell Drugs, adding that he had particularly enjoyed hiring and training employees: "I really enjoyed the human aspect of it, and got a lot of pride out of being able to hire and train people and being able to determine if they'd be successful. Customers perceive it if employees like their job and like working with other people," he explained.

He felt that his greatest challenge came in his first years at Bartell Drugs when he had to earn the trust of George Bartell Jr. "He'd been burned a few times, and we [O'Reilly and I] didn't have years of experience," he elaborated. Other big challenges included modernizing the stores in the 1960s and 1970s and making them competitive. He allowed with a laugh, "It was all challenging. That's what made it fun."

Storrs retired in 2007. In later interviews, he said he believed that one of the keys to Bartell's success is its employees — "people who can give good service and [who] enjoy meeting people."

He added, "I appreciated the honesty and straightforwardness of the company. And I enjoyed working with George Bartell Jr. He was as fair and honest as the day is long. He had confidence in me and allowed me to exercise my decision-making ability over a wide range of situations the company faced. ... In my day we enjoyed businesses who adhered to what was known as the golden rule. People like George Bartell Sr. [and other] merchants who established businesses that endured over many years. I am proud to have been a small part of that experience."

ABOVE: *Val Storrs, ca. 1965.*

OPPOSITE: *George D. Bartell at Bartell's new Magnolia store, 1977.*

selection and quantities of merchandise in their stores to meet their particular clientele's needs.

A Young Entrepreneur

Also in 1973, Bartell's bought an independent drugstore in Greenwood known as Brown's Bi-Rite Drugstore. It was the company's thirteenth store, and its first gain in store count in more than a decade. Though Bartell Drugs had a well-established drugstore a block away, the company feared it was about to lose its lease on that building and wanted to ensure a presence in Greenwood, prompting its purchase of Brown's Bi-Rite. But the lease at Bartell's other store was renewed, making another store a block away unnecessary. The purchased store closed after only three months, but Bartell Drugs bought another thirteenth store in November 1974 in Renton, and this store proved to be more permanent. The company was rebounding.

In the meantime, George D. Bartell was taking a different approach to learning the Bartell business than his father had. Shortly after graduating from college, he approached Storrs and asked for his advice. Storrs recommended that he get more store experience, and Bartell proceeded accordingly, impressing both Storrs and O'Reilly with his willingness to learn the business from the ground up. He informally managed the Brown's Bi-Rite store during the three months it was open in the autumn of 1973, and in 1974 Storrs promoted him to store manager of Bartell's West Seattle store.

The store was older (it opened in 1938) and small by the standards of the mid-1970s. Still, it was a good training ground for Bartell, who, in his words, was "very young to be a manager" at the age of 23. It was at the West Seattle store that he discovered his entrepreneurial side. He looked for opportunities to pass good deals on to customers and discounted items that had been in stock for a while. Sales and profits at the store increased, and management at the office on Boren Avenue noticed.

It also was a learning experience for Bartell. He was not as shy as his father, but people skills did not come naturally to him in his early years with the company. He honed these skills at the West Seattle store, aided by occasional tips from Storrs. Bartell also endured a strike during his early years at the store, and he had to hire staff off the street. Not only did the experience teach him how to think fast and creatively in a protracted emergency, it also gave him a crash course in human resources. By 1977 he was well-prepared for the company's next move, which came that spring when it opened a store in Seattle's Magnolia neighborhood.

A New Store in Magnolia

Bartell Drugs had been interested in a store in Magnolia for some time. It was an established neighborhood with a solid customer base. The biggest risk was that the three drugstores already in Magnolia would provide stiff competition. It was a risk the company was willing to take, and Bartell's Magnolia store opened in April 1977. George D. Bartell was named manager. It was a perfect fit, since he had grown up in Magnolia and already knew some of the new store's customers. He would remain at the store for more than a year before departing for Harvard Business School in 1978.

The Magnolia store was a catalyst. It was the most successful new store opening for Bartell Drugs in more than twenty years, adding strength to the company and giving it the confidence to begin expanding more aggressively. Bartell's added three more stores in 1979 — in Shoreline, Burien, and Kirkland — and ended the 1970s with seventeen stores. More significantly, the Bartell brand that we know today was in place as the decade ended, providing a template for further expansion. Bartell Drugs was perfectly positioned for the economic boom that would come in the 1980s.

Sanford "Sandy" Barnes

Sanford Barnes hailed from North Carolina and had the accent to match. He was a large man and plain spoken, with a fondness for cigars. George D. Bartell has described him as "a pretty big man, but his personality was bigger." Already in his 50s when he started work for Bartell Drugs at its downtown triangle store in the early 1960s, Barnes had previously worked at Tradewell grocery stores and had considerable retail experience. He knew people and enjoyed working with them. Yet he brooked no nonsense. He was the epitome of tough but fair, and left a profound impression on those who knew and worked with him before he retired in 1979.

"There was never a person who taught me more about retail or life than Sandy Barnes," recalled Gordon O' Reilly. "If you didn't do your job, you were gone. But if you did, he was great." He was a people person before the term came into vogue, a man who would sit down with his employees and coach them. But it wasn't just what he did, but how he did it. He was a buoyant, confident man whose positive attitude was infectious. It instilled a respect in those he worked with that still resonates with them today. Before long he was training most store employees who were prospective managers, including George and Jean Bartell.

Barnes was a salesman, and perfectly suited for such a high-traffic location as the triangle store. When customers came in to buy a pack of cigarettes — and far more people smoked in those days — he'd ask them, "Two packs or three?" (O'Reilly later remarked that he was surprised by how often this worked.) When Seafair parades went by the store in August, he'd be outside, cigar in mouth, selling to the crowd. If there was an opportunity, he was there.

Though he liked to sell and liked his customers, he could be as firm with them as he was with his employees. One time he learned there was a peeping tom in a stall in the store's men's room. He filled a pail with water, marched into the restroom, and unceremoniously dumped it over the stall partition onto the voyeur. The occasional drunks who wandered into the store got equally stern treatment from Barnes; he would sometimes escort them out of the store by the napes of their necks.

Shoplifters got the brunt of his wrath. And the triangle store, with pillars inside that made it difficult to see all the way around the store, had its share. Often O'Reilly would catch one and take him back to Barnes. Usually, the shoplifter would beg for mercy. Barnes would thunder in response, "Brother, you're not only a thief, you're a liar too" — and then call the police.

But he did make one exception. One day O'Reilly caught a shoplifter, a young man in his 20s, and took him to Barnes. The man pleaded for mercy, explaining that it was his daughter's birthday and he was getting a few things for her. Opening his coat, the thief revealed a candle and a couple of other small items of nominal value, clearly intended for a young child.

Barnes let him go.

ABOVE LEFT: *Bartell's Ballard store in the 1970s.*

ABOVE RIGHT: *Bartell's Store No. 18 in Kirkland, 1979.*

RIGHT, MIDDLE AND BOTTOM: *Grand opening of Bartell's Magnolia store, April 1977.*

Bartell's Magnolia store interior, 1977.

Sanford "Sandy" Barnes, ca. 1963.

CHAPTER 7

Surging Ahead
(1980–1999)

Sadly, Bartell Drugs announces the biggest sale in Pay'n Save history.

BARTELL DRUGS
TRUSTED SINCE 1890

The 1980s began with a problem that Bartell Drugs had been grappling with for some time: the future of its downtown triangle store. By 1980, the building was forty-five years old and had long been showing its age. For one thing, it leaked. Pigeons roosted on its roof, and on occasion one would die and get stuck in a roof drain, causing more leaks. And the building's interior was old and outdated.

Bartell's had closed most food operations in its stores by 1980. This included its triangle store tearoom (it was replaced by a Frankfurter, a fast-food restaurant specializing in hot dogs), but the store's first-floor soda fountain was still open. It would not survive the year, a victim of newer fast-food chains as well as the looming uncertainty of the Westlake Mall

project. It closed shortly before Christmas, but the closing did not go unnoticed. A warm, nostalgic article about the demise of the old "coffee counters" followed in a March 1981 issue of *Northwest Magazine*, a Sunday magazine that ran in the *Seattle Post-Intelligencer*. Special mention was made in the article of the triangle store fountain's "classic" marble-top counter.

"It's the end of an era," George Bartell Jr. acknowledged when the paper interviewed him. "But this is happening in everything. Everything changes. You can't hang on to the past." Sounding much like his father had nearly thirty years earlier, he added, "Trends change. If you want to keep up in business, you've got to change with them."

WESTLAKE MALL

Bartell was thwarted from making bigger changes to the store by the Westlake Mall project. The idea of developing Westlake — where the triangle store was located — into an urban park with commercial and retail outlets had been first suggested in the 1960s to breathe new life into Seattle's downtown. Years of litigation

OPPOSITE: *Flyover picture of Bartell employees forming "100" in celebration of Bartell's 100th anniversary, 1990.*

ABOVE: *Bartell ad announcing the end of Pay'n Save and inviting its shoppers to Bartell Drugs, 1992.*

followed. The continuing uncertainty of whether there would even be a building on the site kept Bartell Drugs from obtaining needed repairs and replacements to the building and equipment.

By 1980, the City of Seattle was threatening to condemn the property and convert the land into a park as part of the overall project. Litigation to try to prevent this dragged on until 1985. Bartell Drugs and its triangle store found themselves caught in the middle; a March 1982 *Seattle Times* article referred to the building as "long a pawn in the Westlake Mall dispute." But Bartell's soon had to deal with a more immediate problem when it became embroiled in a disagreement with its landlord over the terms of its lease. The dispute ended up in court, and Bartell Drugs lost. This resulted in the closing of the triangle store in April 1984. For many years it had been the highest-volume store in the company, and had played a key role in helping Bartell's survive the difficult days of the 1950s and early 1960s.

The store moved to the nearby Medical Dental building on 5th Avenue. The old triangle building briefly became home to an office supply store, then a bookstore. However, in 1985 the state Supreme Court ruled that the City could condemn the property. The old building was soon torn down and replaced by a park, today known as Westlake Park. The southern end of the monorail, which had been next to the triangle store, was relocated across Pine Street to end at the new Westlake Center, which opened in 1988.

George D. Bartell Returns

George D. Bartell graduated from Harvard Business School in 1980 and returned to Bartell Drugs. Unlike his father, who had been assigned specific job roles in his early years with the company, young Bartell had no specific role when he returned to Seattle. "My dad did not really manage my career," he later explained. "I had to chart my own job." This he did, primarily by reviewing the company's operations and picking up on things that needed to be done as the company began to grow more rapidly.

And there were many things to be done. Bartell Drugs was growing from a relatively small company to a much larger one. As a result, Bartell had plenty to do. He wrote manuals, provided financial analyses when the company considered moving a store or buying a new one, and took part in store design and layout. He also became increasingly active in negotiations when the company purchased new stores.

Five Stores in a Day

Bartell Drugs continued to enjoy steady growth during the early 1980s, with new stores opened in 1981 in Bellevue and Burien, followed by new stores in Kirkland and Des Moines in 1983. However, in 1984 Bartell's opened five new stores — all in one day.

Shoppers Drug Mart, a Canadian chain, had opened five drugstores in King and southern Snohomish counties during the preceding several years. Representatives from the company approached George Bartell Jr. several times during the early 1980s to discuss whether he was interested in selling Bartell Drugs, hoping to use its stores as a springboard to establish a more dominant presence in the Seattle area. He wasn't, but politely told Shoppers to let him know if it ever decided to close its local operations.

In 1984, it did. Bartell's bought the five stores and opened them all on September 7, 1984. One store was in King County, but the other four were in southern Snohomish County — Everett, Mountlake Terrace, and two in Lynnwood. It was a dramatic move, and signaled an increasing boldness and confidence within Bartell Drugs. With these openings, the company's total store count leapt to twenty-six, passing its previous high of twenty-three in 1956.

Two New Headquarters

By 1985, Bartell's corporate office and warehouse on Boren Avenue were no longer big enough for the now rapidly expanding company. The company wanted to keep these operations together, but at the same time needed good road access for shipping. In April 1985, Bartell Drugs moved them to 4930 3rd Avenue S in Seattle, expecting that this location would fill its needs for years to come.

Instead, Bartell's was there for less than five years. By 1989, the company recognized that its continued rapid growth, combined with its expansion plans for the 1990s, would require a larger building for its warehouse and headquarters. In January 1990, Bartell's moved them two blocks away to 4727 Denver Avenue S.

Vic Condiotty / Seattle Times

Jim Mar, manager of the new Bartell drug store in University Village, looks over his domain from his office on the second floor.

Bartell Drugs embarks on expansion

Local competitor edged out by family-controlled firm

by Janice Hayes
Times business reporter

George H. Bartell Jr., president of Bartell Drugs, used to know all of the executives at Pay'n Save by their first names. After all, they had a lot in common. Both were local companies that had made a name for themselves in Seattle's drug-store business.

That has changed. While Bartells has grown gradually in the 97 years since Bartell's father, George Sr., opened a small store at 29th Avenue and Jackson Street, the much larger Pay'n Save has been shuffling managers and is no longer totally locally owned.

"We barely know anyone over there anymore," said Bartell. "We used to know every move they were making."

It's just one sign that the drug business in Seattle is changing.

Discount drug stores, such as Drug Emporium and Fred Meyer, are creating more price competition, making it harder for smaller chains to compete.

Pay 'n Save was a Seattle public company until 1984 when it was bought out by Eddie and Julius Trump, two New York brothers. Last year, the Trumps took the company public again. William Zimmerman, the retired founder of Pic' n' Save, bought 40.6 percent of the company, and attempted to turn Pay'n Save into a discount chain, but the concept didn't work. The company said at its annual meeting in Seattle last week that it would return to a "back-to-basics" merchandising.

Pay'n Save reported a $8.6 million or 51-cent per-share loss for the second quarter ended May 2. The company has 106 stores in the Northwest.

Meanwhile, the Bartells said sales at their 28-store, family-owned drug chain picked up marginally as a result of Pay 'n Save's problems. But the Bartells said it is hard to calculate exactly how much.

"Customers don't walk into our store and say, 'I used to be a Pay'n Save customer'," said George D. Bartell, executive vice president, and son of George H. Bartell. "It's not the kind of thing that is easy to track."

Bartell's University Village store, the

Please see **BARTELL** on H 6

LEFT: *An article in* The Seattle Times *on June 25, 1987, discussed Pay'n Save's difficulties and Bartell's expansion.*

ABOVE: *Bartell Drugs 1916 Boren Avenue headquarters, 1985. Bartell Drugs moved its headquarters shortly after this picture was taken, after having been on this Boren Avenue block for more than seventy years.*

A LANDMARK UNIVERSITY VILLAGE STORE

The company had a banner year in 1987. If there's one year that can be pointed to as the year Bartell Drugs reestablished itself as a dominant force in the Seattle-area pharmacy market, 1987 is that year. The biggest development came early that summer, when the company opened a new store at the University Village shopping center in Seattle that was unlike any it had opened before.

In 1986, the shopping center offered Bartell Drugs a lease in a space that was then occupied by a Pay'n Save drugstore. Bartell Drugs was initially surprised by this offer. Pay'n Save's heyday was passing by 1986, although its store at University Village was still considered to be very good. Bartell management met with shopping center representatives to discuss this offer. The University Village representatives explained that they liked Bartell's upscale image and wanted it for the shopping center. After some negotiations, Bartell Drugs got the lease.

The transition from Pay'n Save to Bartell Drugs did not go smoothly. Pay'n Save had been at University Village for twenty years, and claimed that it had been given no opportunity to renew its lease. The company tried to sublease a space at the shopping center from one of its sister companies, Lamonts (an apparel store), but was rebuffed by University Village. The dispute ended up in court, but Pay'n Save lost. There was so much contention that the judge said she was prepared to issue an injunction to enforce her decision if it became necessary. A few weeks later, Pay'n Save moved out.

Bartell Drugs opened its new store in late June 1987, after a massive, quarter-million-dollar remodel that was compressed into ten days. The store was eighteen thousand square feet, nearly double the size of its typical store. But there was more to it than that. The new store was a bold opportunity to raise the company's visibility and to put it into a bigger league. George D. Bartell told

Jean Bartell Barber's East Coast Years

In 1979, Jean Bartell left Seattle to pursue an MBA at The Wharton School of the University of Pennsylvania in Philadelphia. She later described her two years at Wharton as a turning point in her life. "I'd been in Seattle most of my life... [but this] was a totally different experience. I went to school with people from all over the world. It gave me much more of a world-view than I otherwise would've had if I'd stayed in Seattle," she explained.

She graduated with distinction from Wharton in 1981. She briefly returned to Seattle, but not for long. She'd met Dave Barber at Wharton, and they became engaged in the summer of 1981. They were married the following April and settled in Charlotte, North Carolina, where Barber had a job with North Carolina National Bank (NCNB), then one of the Southeast's leading banks.

Jean Bartell Barber likewise joined NCNB, though in a different department than her husband's. She later explained why she took such a different career path in her early years than her brother and father had taken. She'd always gotten good reviews when she worked for Bartell Drugs and Henbart. But those were her father's companies, and she wondered if she was being given preferential treatment. She wanted to make her own mark.

She was provided with a unique opportunity to do just that at NCNB when she became involved in the vanguard of interstate banking. NCNB had always been aggressive in acquiring other state banks, and by the late 1970s, it was looking to expand outside the state. But it had a problem: Interstate banking was prohibited. However, in 1981 NCNB discovered a legal loophole that allowed it to purchase a bank in Florida, and in January 1982 it bought its first bank in the Sunshine State. It was the first out-of-state acquisition by any bank, but it was only the beginning.

Jean Barber arrived at NCNB in the spring of 1982 and went to work in the bank's balance sheet management department. A few months after she arrived, NCNB acquired two more banks in Florida. Her job was to review these banks' financial statements and make income projections based on contingencies such as interest rates. She rose to become assistant vice president in her department before leaving NCNB three years later.

In 1985, the Barbers moved to Durham, North Carolina. Dave and a partner had opened a home-building business there several years earlier. He'd helped manage the business from Charlotte for the first few years, but in 1985 became more fully involved in the company. Jean worked as treasurer for the company, cutting back to part time after her daughter, Evelyn, was born in 1987. A son, Hugh, followed in 1988. Another son, Neal, arrived in 1991, a year after the Barbers left North Carolina.

NCNB continued to grow through a series of acquisitions and mergers. In 1998, it purchased the Bank of America and adopted its name. Meanwhile, the Barbers moved to Seattle in 1990 to be closer to Jean's family. In 1993, she began work for Bartell Drugs.

LEFT: *Jean Bartell and David Barber on their wedding day, April 17, 1982.*
RIGHT: *Jean Bartell Barber in Charlotte, NC, ca. 1982.*

The Seattle Times that the store was a test site to see if the company could successfully run a larger store in a shopping center.

The company soon found that it could. Its market share jumped. The press took notice. More importantly, so did its customers, who before long were shopping at the store in greater numbers than Pay'n Save had achieved at the same location. The acquisition of the University Village store gave Bartell Drugs the confidence to open similar, larger stores in the ensuing years.

Also in 1987, the company moved its West Seattle store into Jefferson Square, a mixed-use development that also had apartments and an office building. It was the first Bartell venture into a mixed-use development (as opposed to a strictly retail location) but would prove so successful that it would not be the last.

The 1980s drew to a close with another Bartell wedding. On November 4, 1989, George D. Bartell married June Erdman, a dietitian. They had two children: Claire, born in 1994, and Mike, born in 1997.

GEORGE D. BARTELL BECOMES PRESIDENT

George Bartell Jr. had decided to step down as president before 1990 dawned, and felt that the company's centennial that year was the perfect time for it. With the exception of his four-year hiatus during World War II, he had been president of Bartell Drugs for fifty years. It was a remarkable experience for Bartell. He became president almost precisely when the company reached its first pinnacle of success, and for the first half of his presidency weathered a series of contractions and management changes that other companies might not have survived. Then, at the midpoint of his presidency, he rejuvenated the company's management team with the right mix of talent, eventually leading to Bartell Drugs coming back bigger and better than before.

On April 1, 1990, George D. Bartell, then 38, succeeded his father as president of the Bartell Drug Company. He had gradually taken on a more assertive role in the company's operations during the 1980s, and by 1987 had become executive vice president. He'd impressed the company's management team with his drive, but also with his intuition of what was needed to make Bartell Drugs more successful while remaining responsive to its customers. More aggressive than his father, the younger Bartell was well-prepared

ABOVE: *George D. and June Bartell on their wedding day, November 4, 1989.*

LEFT: *George Bartell Jr. and George D. Bartell, 1990.*

in experience and temperament to lead the company by 1990. And unlike the early years of George Bartell Jr.'s presidency, when he had been largely overshadowed by the senior Bartell, there was little question after April 1990 that George D. Bartell was in charge. That said, he was not reticent about asking his father for advice.

The Bartell Drugs centennial in 1990 was a yearlong celebration that involved many of its 750 employees, and was full of activities, promotions, and sales events. Birthday cakes were served periodically at its stores during the year, and in August a drawing was held at each of Bartell's thirty-three stores for an 1890 silver dollar. A community transit bus was painted robin's-egg blue with drawings representing Bartell customers over the preceding one hundred years on the sides of the bus. Painted hats adorned the bus windows. With a little imagination, someone glancing at the passengers as the bus passed could visualize a rider representing a Bartell customer from over the years. It was hard to miss on the streets of Seattle.

BIGGER STORES, NEW LOCATIONS

During the 1980s, Bartell's growth had come from acquisitions of existing drugstores and from opening new stores in new shopping developments. However, Bartell Drugs modified its growth strategy for much of the 1990s. The success at its big University Village store had shown the company that it could compete with its larger rivals. To meet this challenge, Bartell Drugs expanded some of its already well-established stores. For example, the Magnolia store moved into a bigger building in 1992, and a remodel of the Ballard store in the early 1990s doubled its size. In 1995, Bartell's Queen Anne store moved into a larger space that was located above a Larry's Market, a high-end grocery store. Bartell's took the opportunity of the move to make this store Seattle's first modern twenty-four-hour drugstore.

LEFT TOP: *Bartell's Store No. 2 at its new location in the Crossroads Shopping Center in Bellevue, 1981.*

CENTER: *One of the five new stores purchased by Bartell Drugs from Shoppers Drug Mart in 1984; Store No. 25 at Silverlake in Everett.*

BOTTOM: *Another Bartell purchase from Shoppers: Store No. 27 in Lynnwood.*

Bartell's centennial bus, 1990. This Seattle Metro bus, sponsored by Bartell Drugs to promote its centennial, was hard to miss on the streets of downtown Seattle.

Another strategic change came in 1990, when Bartell Drugs hired Jean Barber's husband, Dave, as the company's first director of real estate. Dave was a Wharton graduate with a concentration in real estate, and he had gained further real estate experience before coming to Bartell's.

The company opened fourteen new stores during the 1990s, including a few in new locations. Bartell Drugs moved into Pierce County in October 1991, when it opened a store in the Olympic Village Shopping Center in Gig Harbor. This was initially thought to be a bit of a gamble since the store was south of what the company considered to be its traditional trading area. But the gamble paid off, and more than twenty years later this store continues to operate in its original location.

The new Gig Harbor store also offered one-hour in-store photo processing, leading the way in the return of photo laboratories to Bartell Drugs after a thirty-year hiatus. "[We] sell lots of film, for some reason. We always have," observed George D. Bartell in a subsequent interview, so it made sense to add on-site developing. These new labs were much smaller than the original Bartell photo lab on Boren Avenue, and they each operated in individual stores. Bartell's gradually added one-hour photo labs to more stores during the 1990s, and by 2002 had them in most of its stores.

JEAN BARTELL BARBER JOINS BARTELL DRUGS

Jean Barber and her family moved to Seattle in 1990. She concentrated on raising her growing family for a few years, but by 1993 she was restless. She began working part time for Bartell Drugs that year, handling the company's risk management and property/liability insurance program. She also served as a one-person technology department for Bartell Drugs, buying new computers and getting them serviced as needed. In addition, she became manager of Henbart (Bartell's commercial real estate investment company) in 1993 and served in this position for about fifteen years.

In 1997, she was promoted to chief financial officer. Her duties broadened to include handling the company's financial analyses, its treasury functions, and its cash flow projections. Her banking experience also prompted her to bring more diversity to the company's financial plan. "I knew that the Bartell way wasn't the only way. Things change, our marketplace evolves, so we need to evolve with it," she explained in a 2005 interview

Barber's duties later expanded to include heading the company's strategic planning. She also took on oversight of Bartell's human resources department. In 2006, her title changed to vice chairman and treasurer to better reflect her role in the company.

Point-of-Sale Scanning

In 1995, Bartell Drugs began installing point-of-sale (POS) scanning in its stores. POS scanning is a centralized system where all the scanners in a store — often a dozen or more — report to a centralized database. It was a $5 million project that took three years to fully implement.

Before point-of-sale scanning arrived, every piece of merchandise in every Bartell store had a price ticket. These had to be manually changed every time the price changed on an item, which was a labor-intensive chore. And on occasion a customer would remove a price ticket from a cheaper item, put it on a more expensive item, and check out. This not only resulted in lost revenues but also made inventory management more difficult.

The POS system changed all that. With just a few keystrokes, price changes could now be input into a computer in Bartell's corporate office, and the barcode tag that was on every piece of merchandise would automatically reflect this new price. It was no longer necessary to change individual merchandise tags every time the price changed. A new shelf tag, which showed the item's price, would be printed automatically to go on the shelf edge in front of every row of merchandise.

The POS system made it easier to track sales, letting employees know at a glance an item's sales history. It could also alert employees when a product was running low, so they could quickly order more. Best of all, the system allowed many aspects of a store's operations to be connected and operated within a single integrated system. This not only saved time but also made tracking of store operations more accurate and efficient.

Gifts and Hardware

With the exception of its food and photo operations, Bartell Drugs had concentrated on its pharmacy operations and the sale of over-the-counter drugs for most of its history, believing that expansion into other retail areas would dilute its focus and potentially weaken the company. Bartell management watched something similar happen to Pay'n Save during the 1980s (though other factors, including a minority shareholder issue analogous to the one Bartell Drugs faced in the 1960s, also contributed to its eventual demise). That approach changed — slightly — in 1987.

That year Bartell Drugs moved its West Seattle store to a new location a couple of blocks away. It still had two months left on its lease at the old location and opted to open a stationery store there for that period. This was only intended to be temporary, which was probably a good thing since the venture was not successful. Yet the experience did not entirely dissuade the company from considering other new opportunities when they came up.

Such an opportunity arose in 1995, when Bartell's acquired a drugstore in Lake Stevens. This drugstore had also operated as a gift store that had been popular with customers, and Bartell Drugs kept it. Likewise, the company bought a store in Snohomish in 1997 that had been a combination drugstore and True Value hardware store, and kept the hardware operation. More than fifteen years later, the operations in these two stores continue to do well, perhaps because they are so popular with that particular customer base. However, Bartell's has not made a concerted effort to expand into other areas of retail.

The company tested other new ideas in the 1990s. In 1998, it opened its first drive-through pharmacy at a new store in Renton. As with some of its other ventures, Bartell's considered this first drive-through a test site to see if customers liked it. They did, and the company wasted little time adding drive-throughs to its other new stores when it was feasible. This included a store opened in October 1999 in Marysville, Bartell's northernmost location to date.

New Competitors

Retail pharmacy changed dramatically during the 1980s and 1990s. Bartell's toughest competitor, Pay'n Save, faded from the pharmacy scene, but it was replaced by other rivals, such as Walgreens and Rite Aid. Competition also arose from what had previously been an unlikely competitor, at least during the twentieth century: grocery stores. Albertson's and Safeway were offering pharmacies in their grocery stores by the early 1980s, and this trend accelerated over time. Discount stores such as Kmart and Target also began offering pharmacies. Yet despite the increased competition from a wide variety of competitors, Bartell Drugs prospered.

Pharmacy itself likewise changed significantly. These years — especially the 1990s — saw the arrival of brand-name drugs, such as Lipitor, Paxil, and Prilosec. These drugs were a huge boost

TOP LEFT: *A Halloween candy display store at Bartell's Auburn store in 1995 demonstrates the change during the twentieth century from the sale of freshly-baked candy at Bartell Drugs to processed candy.*

ABOVE LEFT: *Bartell's University Village store, 1990.*

TOP RIGHT: *Bartell Drugs opened its first store in Pierce County when it cut the ribbon for its Gig Harbor store on October 14, 1991. George D. Bartell is on the far right.*

ABOVE RIGHT: *Bartell's grand opening of its Marysville store, October 13, 1999. George Bartell Jr. is directly behind the scissor blades, while George D. Bartell is on the far right.*

to business, leading to some years of double-digit increases to Bartell's pharmacy business in the 1990s. Clinical pharmacy also began to transform Bartell's operations during this decade.

A more subtle change in retail pharmacy was how pharmacies were paid for prescriptions. For much of the twentieth century, customers paid for prescriptions with cash, with an occasional credit purchase. Those fortunate enough to have prescription-drug insurance coverage would submit their prescription charges to their insurer for reimbursement. While there were insurance plans that covered prescriptions in 1980, they didn't play as prominent a role in prescription reimbursement as they would twenty years later. Managed care, with its HMOs and PPOs, was only a blip on the horizon.

The emergence of managed health care in the final two decades of the twentieth century, and in particular the rise of direct-pay third-party prescription plans, changed how drugstores were paid. By the mid-1990s pharmacies found themselves dealing with a variety of these plans, which dictated how much a pharmacy would be paid for a drug. It was a sea change for most pharmacists, who not only had to deal with the increased paperwork these plans required, but also now had to wait for the plans to reimburse them, instead of being paid by customers at the time of purchase.

Bartell Drugs closed the 1990s with forty-five stores in operation and more than thirteen hundred employees. But as the decade ended, other changes were taking place that would transform pharmacy into the modern operation that we now take for granted. Bartell Drugs would integrate these changes into its operations and move confidently into the twenty-first century.

As had his father before him, George Bartell Jr. remained a presence in the Bartell Drug Company after he stepped down as president in 1990. Unlike his father, he did not continue to run the company. He typically worked four and a half days a week, but he had no significant responsibilities. He attended executive and board meetings and often provided advice on larger issues. He served as the company's chairman until 2001, when he was named chairman emeritus.

In his later years as president, he enjoyed making visits every December to each of his stores to thank the employees for their work during the year. He continued this tradition of "Christmas visits" after he resigned, and it was his baby: One year, when his son suggested they do the visits together, Bartell would not hear of it. On occasion he would walk directly into one of the pharmacies to greet employees, sometimes startling newer employees, who didn't recognize him and would stop him to ask why he was there.

He enjoyed play as well as work. He liked traveling and loved hiking in the Cascades. But his true love was golf. He had been an avid golfer since he was a youngster (in his prime he had a handicap of seven), and after his retirement he continued his habit of playing twice a week, on Wednesday

George Bartell Jr.'s Later Years

afternoons and Saturdays. For a few weeks during the winter, he and his wife, Betty, traveled to Palm Springs so he could golf with friends.

As the 1990s progressed, Bartell began to slowly decline from a form of dementia. After Betty Bartell died in 2003, he remained at his home in Seattle for a few more years, assisted by caregivers. He quit working at age 87, though he still enjoyed attending grand openings for new stores and visiting Bartell's other stores when he could. He didn't give up golf until he was 90. However, his health further deteriorated, and in the spring of 2007, his children moved him to an assisted-living facility in Scottsdale, Arizona. He died from pneumonia in Mesa, Arizona, on January 21, 2009.

Bartell participated in a number of civic activities. He served as president of the Municipal League of King County between 1966 and 1968. He served in several positions, including chairman, of the Pacific Northwest Chapter of the Young Presidents Organization, and was a director of the Seattle Retail Trade Bureau and of Greater Seattle, Incorporated. He also was a member of the Rainier Club, the Seattle Golf and Country Club, the Scottish Rite Temple, and the Chief Executive Forum.

FACING PAGE: *George Bartell Jr. golfing at a young age, ca. 1921.*

ABOVE FROM LEFT: *George Bartell Jr. holding a "special edition – Bartell extra" section that appeared in* The Seattle Times *during Bartell's 1990 centennial.*

George Bartell Jr. (shown on the far right) golfing with friends in Yakima, 1977.

George and Betty Bartell at George D. Bartell's wedding, November 4, 1989.

SERVING WEST SEATTLE SINCE 1938

GEO. H. BARTELL

LAKE WASHINGTON PHARMACY

BARTELL DRUGS

BARTELL DRUGS   BARTELL DRUGS

BARTELL DRUGS

4552 California Ave. S.W. · 1938

27th & Jackson

Admiral Way · 2002

BARTELL DRUGS

Washington's Own Drugstores

CHAPTER 8

Meeting the Twenty-First Century
(2000–2014)

"The 1990s were easy years," remarked Jean Barber in a 2013 interview. "They were in no way like the challenges since 2000. The competitive environment was easier, and you weren't always trying to figure out something new you needed to do." Bartell's anticipated some of the challenges, such as integrating the relatively new Internet into its business model, as the new century began. Other challenges were unanticipated, such as one that arose in 2000, when Bartell Drugs found itself thrust into the national spotlight over providing insurance coverage for contraceptives.

It was an ironic twist for Bartell's. In 1998, it had become one of the first chain drugstores in Washington to join a statewide pilot

program to provide emergency contraception prescriptions to women. But the company's employee medical plan did not cover contraceptives for nonunion employees, though they did receive an employee discount for contraceptives. (As part of their contract, union employees received such coverage — but by 2000, there were fewer union employees at Bartell Drugs than there had been in the past.)

In 1999, 26-year-old Jennifer Erickson, head pharmacist at Bartell's Bellevue store, wrote the company's human resources department and asked that Bartell Drugs cover contraceptives in its self-insured health plan. Bartell's eventually declined. Encouraged by Planned Parenthood, Erickson filed a complaint with the Equal Employment Opportunity Commission in December 1999. That was followed in July 2000 by a class-action lawsuit filed against Bartell Drugs in federal court in Seattle by lawyers for Planned Parenthood; the suit was brought in Erickson's name as the lead plaintiff in the case. The complaint alleged that Bartell's prescription benefit plan for nonunion employees violated Title VII of the 1964 Civil Rights Act

OPPOSITE: *A Bartell Drugs mural on a West Seattle wall, November 22, 2002.*

ABOVE: *George D. Bartell and Jean Bartell Barber receiving the Best in the Northwest Washington Family Business Award, November 2006.*

by providing less-complete prescription coverage to its female employees than to its male employees.

The president of Planned Parenthood of Western Washington told *The Seattle Times* that the organization had approached fifty companies in the state to ask that these companies add contraceptive coverage to their insurance plans, and that all had declined. (According to Planned Parenthood, only about half of U.S. employers covered contraceptives at the time.) She candidly added that Planned Parenthood decided to name Bartell Drugs in its lawsuit because Bartell's was considered to be a good employer and a progressive company. Bartell Drugs also may have been considered an attractive target because approximately two-thirds of its employees were women. The case was widely reported in the local and national media, with much of the coverage sympathetic to Planned Parenthood and Erickson.

The case was decided in favor of Erickson and Planned Parenthood in June 2001 and generated national attention. Bartell Drugs was again in the center of an unwelcome media firestorm, even though the company's issue with providing contraceptive coverage had been primarily based on its cost, which was a common reason why many employers did not provide this coverage at the time.

Because Bartell Drugs was self-insured, the ruling did not apply to insurers doing business in Washington. That quickly changed. The next month two groups filed a class-action lawsuit in King County Superior Court against Regence Blue Shield for its failure to provide full coverage for contraceptives in its health policies. Before that case was decided, state Insurance Commissioner Mike Kreidler signed a new administrative regulation requiring insurers to cover birth control in prescription-drug plans issued for Washington policyholders.

THE 9/11 ATTACKS

Kreidler signed the new regulation on September 5, 2001. Six days later, on the morning of Tuesday, September 11, terrorist attacks in New York and Washington, D.C., stunned the nation. Bartell's found itself touched by the tragedy in an unexpected way. All commercial flights in the country were grounded for several days. Travelers found themselves stranded in Seattle with no access to their medications. As they began to realize they were going to be in

Seattle for a while, they began fanning out to drugstores to try to get prescriptions.

Dries Vander Poppen was the head pharmacist at Bartell's Des Moines store, located about two and a half miles south of the airport. When he reported to work at 3 p.m. on September 11, he was greeted by a stack of requests for prescription transfers. Marooned travelers who were staying at the nearby Red Lion Hotel dutifully shuttled down to pick up their prescriptions over the next few days, and Vander Poppen and his staff were kept busy calling doctors and pharmacists all over the country to confirm the prescriptions. It was a challenge, but the multiple transfers ran more smoothly than one might have expected. "Most doctors and pharmacists were understanding and helpful and tended to expedite the requests," Vander Poppen later recalled.

It was a hectic week. Vander Poppen later estimated the store filled more than a hundred prescription transfers. By the end of the week, most of the grounded guests had found flights out of Seattle, but the Des Moines store had left an impression. Some of the travelers sent the store notes when they got home, thanking Bartell's for going the extra mile during the crisis.

TECHNOLOGICAL WIZARDRY

In the mid-1990s, the Internet came on the scene, dazzling many with its potential. Yet it was still a relatively new tool in 2000, and its applications were far more limited than they would be even a decade later. Bartell Drugs had just inaugurated its first website in 1998, and was still making adjustments to it as the new century began. One such adjustment came with online shopping, which was still gaining public acceptance in 2000. Late that year Bartell's launched its first on-line shopping site at bartelldrugs.com, offering prescription refills and more than five thousand health and beauty items. It flopped, partly because Bartell's was a little early in trying this venture, and partly because pharmacy wasn't — and still isn't — a market that easily lends itself to online trade. (For instance, if you need toothpaste, or urgently need medication, you're not going to order it online and wait for it to be delivered.) Still, the Internet has proved to be a valuable tool for the company, letting it advertise online, list employment opportunities, and provide its customers with information about its stores and their products.

Community Recognition

For much of its history Bartell Drugs has been known as a leader in the Puget Sound business community, and over the years both the company and its founder have been recognized for their efforts. In 1997, George Bartell Sr. received special recognition when he was inducted into the Junior Achievement Puget Sound Business Hall of Fame. Since 1987, this partnership between the *Puget Sound Business Journal* and Junior Achievement of Washington has inducted more than one hundred prominent local business leaders based on their contributions to the region's business community.

Bartell Drugs itself received several noteworthy community awards a few years later. In 2001, the company was awarded the eighth annual Best in the Northwest Washington Family Business Award in the Heritage Business category by the Family Enterprise Institute of the Pacific Lutheran University (PLU) School of Business. (This award recognized businesses that had been in operation for more than fifty years.) Five years later, Bartell's received a second honor from PLU when it was awarded the Best in the Northwest Washington Family Business Award in the Large Business category.

In July 2004, the company was presented with the Washington State Century Corporation Award by Secretary of State Sam Reed in a ceremony timed to coincide with the opening of Bartell's new store at 4th Avenue and Madison Street in Seattle. One hundred years after its incorporation, Bartell Drugs was one of only forty-three businesses remaining from the eight hundred incorporated in Washington in 1904.

Bartell's has always believed that its employees deserve credit for the company's success, and some of these employees have also received awards for their work. One recent example dates from 2011, when Chief Operating Officer Ed Littleton, a twenty-year veteran of Bartell Drugs, received the National Association of Chain Drug Stores Harold W. Pratt Award. Considered to be community pharmacy's highest honor, this award recognizes individuals who have contributed to the promotion, recognition, and improvement of pharmacy practice in the chain drug industry.

Bartell Century Corporation award, 2004.

TOP: *Jean Barber, George Bartell Jr., and George D. Bartell, ca. 2003.*
ABOVE: *Bartell Store No. 61 at 4th Avenue and Madison Street, ca. 2010.*

Advances in computer software also benefited Bartell's operations. In the early 2000s, Bartell's began using planograms, software that allowed management to create a computer screen snapshot of a display shelf to better plan its store displays. About the same time, the company started using a new inventory management program that let its staff craft customized reports to better track the sale and inventory levels of products in Bartell stores. This let the buyers more easily see what was selling well and helped them better prepare their orders. That was followed by an automated replenishment system, software that allowed the company to set minimum levels of inventory for its pharmaceutical products. Once the inventory for a particular product dropped below a certain level, the system automatically reordered it. All of these changes have been a big help to the company in handling its merchandise from first purchase to final sale.

DIGITAL PHOTO LABS

By the early years of the new century, digital cameras were gaining in popularity. In 2003 Bartell Drugs launched digital photo processing in its stores, becoming one of the first major retailers in the Puget Sound area to offer it. It was a quantum leap forward in handling photographs, because it let customers play a direct role in printing their own pictures. Customers could sit at one of the photo kiosks at a Bartell store, insert a memory card or USB flash drive into the machine, and follow the screen prompts to print out their own pictures within minutes. Or they could scan pictures they already had. The technology allowed customers to enhance or crop their pictures, and they could create holiday cards from their pictures. Other advances in technology enabled Bartell customers sitting at a kiosk to access their pictures from online sharing sites such as Facebook to create not only pictures, but movie DVDs and other products.

Bartell's took this a step further in 2011, when it implemented the Kodak Adaptive Picture Exchange system in most of its digital photo labs. This not only allowed for in-store digital processing but it let customers create and order photo products (calendars and double-sided photo books are two examples) from home via the Internet that could be downloaded and printed at a Bartell store.

STEADY GROWTH

Bartell's continued its steady growth the early years of the new century. The company opened its fiftieth store in January 2001 in Tacoma, its first location in that city and only its second in Pierce County. A third Pierce County store followed in 2002 in University Place. In Seattle, the company relocated its University Village store to a new, 20,500-square-foot store in 2003, and also opened a new store in Edmonds that year.

Other new stores followed in 2004 in Bellevue and downtown Seattle. The new Bellevue store was the Eastside's first twenty-four-hour store, while Bartell's new downtown store, opened in July on the corner of 4th Avenue and Madison Street, was one of its most attractive stores yet. A former bank branch, the store had large, high windows and a twenty-four-foot-high vaulted ceiling lobby. The store also featured an espresso bar — Bartell's first, and a nod toward Seattle's fondness for upscale coffee. In keeping with the company's practice of stocking its stores with products geared toward the customers in each store's neighborhood, this store had a higher stock of convenience foods and soft drinks — a decision that was appreciated by office workers and others downtown in need of a quick, hassle-free snack.

Another notable store opening came in November 2005 in Stanwood, located in northwestern Snohomish County. It was Bartell's northernmost location yet, and a further expansion of its traditional Puget Sound base. Bartell's introduced itself to the community by hosting a celebration at the store, featuring a bratwurst fry, live music, and free wagon rides. Even J.P. Patches, a kindly clown who delighted hundreds of thousands of Western Washington youngsters with his television show between 1958 and 1981, made a cameo appearance.

The Great Recession, America's worst economic downturn since the Great Depression of the 1930s, began in December 2007 and its effects reverberated for several years. The slowdown affected Bartell Drugs as it did other businesses, but Bartell's was more fortunate than many. As had been the case during the Great Depression, its stores sold products that people needed. Though it would be an overstatement to say Bartell's flourished during the Great Recession, as it had during the Great Depression, the downturn never threatened the company's stability.

TOP: *Val Storrs congratulates a store employee at the opening of Store No. 54 in Tacoma on January 24, 2001.*

ABOVE: *Well-known clown J.P. Patches was on hand to celebrate Bartell's opening of its Stanwood store in November 2005.*

1938

1948

BARTELL'S UNIVERSITY DISTRICT STORE № 11

BARTELL DRUGS HAS BEEN ON (OR NEAR) THE SOUTHEAST CORNER OF NE 45TH STREET AND UNIVERSITY WAY SINCE 1926, BY FAR ITS LONGEST PRESENCE IN ONE PLACE.

2002

1975

The retirement of Gordon O'Reilly in 2003 and Val Storrs in 2007 led to Bartell Drugs hiring a new generation of executives. Many of them came from outside Bartell's, and brought needed expertise in areas like merchandising, marketing, human resources, and pharmacy. Others were promoted from within. In 2010, Bartell Drugs also added an outside board of directors for the first time since the 1960s. These executives have brought new ideas and strategic thinking that are needed to handle the challenges of modern retailing.

In October 2012, Bartell Drugs moved its corporate office to 4025 Delridge Way SW in West Seattle. (The company warehouse remained in Seattle's industrial area at 4140 East Marginal Way S, where it had been since 2005.) The corporate office's move was one to more pleasant surroundings, but, as with most Bartell decisions, there was a practical reason for the move — the new building had fiber optic capabilities, which the old building lacked.

CLINICAL PHARMACY

By 2000, clinical pharmacy was transforming pharmacies into places where one could get not only medicine but some forms of medical treatment as well. To some extent, this transformation brings to mind Washington Territory's earliest days, when many of its pharmacists were also physicians. Although Bartell pharmacists aren't doctors, many of them can provide services that would have been unimaginable to a territorial physician 150 years ago.

The American College of Clinical Pharmacy defines clinical pharmacy as "a health science discipline in which pharmacists provide patient care that optimizes medication therapy and promotes health, wellness, and disease prevention." Thus, the role of the pharmacist has expanded in recent decades to include other services that previously had been offered only by physicians or nurse practitioners. But clinical pharmacy is not new. It first arose

in the United States in the 1940s and slowly became more widespread, first in hospitals and then in community pharmacies. By the late 1970s, pharmacy customers could do such things as check their blood pressure on a monitor when they went to the drugstore.

In 1979, Washington became one of the first states in the country to enact legislation to allow pharmacists to participate in collaborative drug therapy agreements with physicians. As in all states that allow pharmacists to prescribe medications, pharmacists in Washington must cosign a complete prescribing protocol with a licensed practitioner, which must then be approved by the Washington State Board of Pharmacy. Pharmacists can then write prescriptions, discuss the effects of these prescriptions with their customers, and provide medication management. They can also order laboratory tests in order to monitor and evaluate.

Clinical pharmacy played a relatively small part of the pharmacist's role at Bartell Drugs until the 1990s, when it began to expand more rapidly. This was in part related to changes in requirements for a pharmacy degree, which, beginning in the 1990s, required an extra year of schooling. The advantage of this extra training was that it allowed community pharmacists to provide services that previously had only been provided in hospitals. For example, by 2000 you could not only have your blood pressure monitored at a Bartell Drugs, you could have your bone density tested too.

Immunizations are perhaps the most salient example of clinical pharmacy, and Bartell's took the lead as the first pharmacy in the state to offer them. These immunizations extend far beyond the well-known flu shot. Bartell's can also give vaccines for shingles, pneumonia, whooping cough, and even rabies. This convenience has not been lost on Bartell customers, to the point that many customers get them there instead of going to their doctor. Bartell's also offers travel clinics in many of its stores where customers can get travel-related information and immunizations for such diseases as yellow fever and typhoid.

It hasn't stopped there. Bartell's is seeking to expand its protocols, so it can provide more services. One of the more interesting ones is a recently obtained protocol to fill veterinary prescriptions, which allows Bartell stores to dispense pet medications. In a way, it's a throwback to Bartell Drugs' earliest years, when George Bartell Sr. sold horse medicines at his little store on Jackson Street.

FACING PAGE CLOCKWISE FROM LEFT: *Bartell's University District store in the lower right, 1938. The store moved next door to the corner in the 1940s, and in 1986, the store expanded to include its original location.*

A shot from the late 1940s showing the University District store in its present location.

Bartell's University District store, ca. 1975.

Bartell's University District store, June 14, 2002.

Aside from convenience, another big benefit to clinical pharmacy is reduced health costs, since the patient doesn't need to see a physician. Moreover, other benefits, such as lower rates of adverse drug reactions and shortened hospital stays, have been documented.

GENERIC DRUGS ARRIVE

The rise of generic drugs in the early twenty-first century has, in some ways, made pharmacy operations more challenging. Once touted as an economic savior, some generic drugs have now become so inexpensive that it's hard for a drugstore to make any money selling them. This is more of a threat to smaller,

independent pharmacies that depend almost entirely on the sale of pharmaceuticals for their livelihood. Larger pharmacies that offer more retail lines have not been as significantly affected, though they too have felt the pinch.

Retail pharmacy today is a business that is far different than George Bartell's first drugstore in 1890. In today's Bartell drugstore you can find all kinds of over-the-counter medicines, from cold remedies and eye drops to hair-regrowth products. You can buy other items too, such as compact discs, flash drives, and USB cables for your computer. You can even buy nonstick cooking spray for frying pans and the pans themselves. A trip to a Bartell store today is one that even the energetic and optimistic George Bartell

Bartell Drugs often updates and remodels its stores as the above pictures of the Lake Sammamish store show. The two on the left were taken in May 2012, the two on the right in August 2013.

Community Service

Bartell Drugs knows that its success is linked to the vitality of the communities it serves, and the company has a long history of giving back. Indeed, by 2002, Bartell Drugs was supporting more than seventy organizations and community events annually. Some of the events that Bartell's has sponsored over the years include the Wallingford Pumpkin Push, an annual run held to raise funds for the 45th Street Clinic; Smile Days, an event designed to give the King County Dental Society a chance to provide free dental screenings for children; and the Teddy Bear Patrol.

The Teddy Bear Patrol has become a favorite with Bartell customers. Every year Bartell Drugs teams up with an area radio station to help collect teddy bears, which are then distributed to emergency responders to help calm a scared child in a crisis. Bartell stores serve as a drop-off point for donations (or you can buy and donate a "Bartell Bear" and Bartell's will match your donation), and its customers have responded: In 2001 alone, more than twenty thousand bears were collected.

The company has also been fast to respond after a tragedy. After the 2001 terrorist attacks, Bartell's launched a drive to help raise funds for a number of charitable organizations such as the Salvation Army, Northwest Harvest, and the Union Gospel Mission. Following the 2004 Indian Ocean tsunami that killed more than two hundred thousand people, the company partnered with the Moyer Foundation to raise funds for children orphaned by the tsunami. In four months Bartell's raised more than $47,000, part of which came from its store sales of the foundation's "Care For Each Other" bracelets. More recently, Bartell's has collected money in partnership with the Salvation Army for the Oso slide victims.

Bartell Drugs has redirected its support in recent years to organizations that it believes will benefit the most. Some of the organizations it supports in 2014 are as varied as the Pacific Science Center, the Washington Poison Center, and HistoryLink.org, the online encyclopedia of Washington State history. But Bartell's lets its customers choose, too. One of its latest efforts is the introduction of a 'B' Caring Card, a fund-raising card that allows a customer to donate up to 4 percent of his purchase amount to a qualified organization of his choice.

TOP: *Every year Bartell Drugs teams up with an area radio station to help collect teddy bears, which are then distributed to emergency responders to help calm a scared child in a crisis. Pictured here is the 2013 "teddy bear patrol" consisting of members of the Des Moines police and radio station WARM 106.9, March 2013.*

TOP: *The Barber family at son Hugh's graduation from Rhodes college, June 2011. From left: Neal, Jean, Hugh, Evelyn, and Dave Barber.*

BELOW: *The George D. Bartell family at the opening of Bartell's Lake Union store, August 6, 2013. From left: Claire, Mike, June and George D. Bartell.*

Sr. would not have dreamed of in 1890. But in a flashback to yesteryear — indeed, yestercentury — Bartell drugstores still sell witch hazel.

THE NEXT BARTELL GENERATION

It was a sad day when George Bartell Jr. died on January 21, 2009. "He was the consummate gentleman," said George D. Bartell at the memorial service, and many agreed. Left with a big act to follow after his father, George Bartell Jr. had made his mark as the second-generation Bartell when he guided the company back from the brink in the 1960s, and he left the company in an even stronger position than it had been in when he became president in 1939.

At present, the third-generation Bartells are both in their early 60s. Although George Bartell and Jean Barber have no immediate plans to retire, they aren't oblivious to the march of time. Both allow that they may begin cutting back their duties when they reach their mid-60s and not be involved in as many critical roles as they are today. At the same time, they're quick to emphasize that they intend to remain active and relevant in the company. Given that both of their parents lived into their 90s, it's not unreasonable to expect that we'll be hearing from them both for years to come.

Inevitably, people ask about the next Bartell generation. After all, Bartell has two children, and Barber has three. At this writing, Bartell's daughter Claire is 20 years old and son Mike is a teenager, and their career plans are largely a blank slate. However, Barber's three children are all in their 20s and launching or preparing to launch careers. While none of them currently work for Bartell Drugs, that doesn't mean that one or more of them may not someday.

As the fourth Bartell generation grew up, their parents gradually began exposing them more to the company, and eventually implemented an informal training program for them. This training program includes an internship that is designed around a particular area of interest — for example, Barber's daughter Evelyn participated in a nine-month company internship in 2010 and 2011 that had modules in marketing and merchandising, while her son Hugh is considering an internship in 2015 that will likewise be designed around his interests. The internships include exposure to other facets of the company to provide the fullest picture possible. "The goal is to allow our kids to evaluate our family business as a whole and see if they want to pursue a role in part of it," explains Barber. "In fact, we expect Evie (Evelyn) to join the company in 2015."

To the Future

George Bartell Sr. always said that Bartell Drugs was a Seattle institution, but by the time he died, he realized that Seattle was expanding into Greater Seattle. Both his son and grandson continued the company's expansion, gradually opening stores farther and farther away from downtown Seattle as development in the Puget Sound region similarly expanded. But both George Bartell Jr. and George D. Bartell continued to maintain that Bartell's is a Puget Sound company, with no broader ambitions.

The family still has that philosophy today. "Our family has always been committed to serving this region and providing a significant number of jobs," explains Barber. (In May 2014, Bartell Drugs has more than seventeen hundred employees in sixty-three locations and its corporate office.) Echoing her grand-father, she adds, "Our money has always been reinvested here."

Bartell admits to having occasionally thought of expanding into other counties in Western Washington, maybe even east of the Cascades. But he swiftly adds that the company's focus will remain on the Puget Sound region. He points out that Bartell Drugs' philosophy is broader than expansion just for the sake of growth: "We're focused on the greater good. It makes it all worthwhile."

TOP: *The Bartell Drugs warehouse, 2012.*

BELOW: *"Bart" — a nickname for "Bartell's historic delivery truck" — often appears at grand openings, such as the one shown here near Lake Serene in Lynnwood on July 21, 2009.*

№ 9

HEADQUARTERS

№ 39

№ 31

A SAMPLING OF BARTELL DRUG STORES

BARTELL'S STORE No. 9 ~ GREENWOOD. 2010.

BARTELL'S HEADQUARTERS ~ WEST SEATTLE, 2014.

BARTELL'S STORE No. 66 ~ LAKE CITY, 2008.

BARTELL'S STORE No. 29 ~ SAMMAMISH, 2014.

BARTELL'S STORE No. 58 ~ EDMONDS, 2003.

BARTELL'S STORE No. 31 ~ UNIVERSITY VILLAGE, 2010.

BARTELL'S STORE No. 39 ~ GIG HARBOR, 2010.

Chronology

December 14, 1868 George Bartell Sr. is born in Dickinson County, Kansas.

1883 Bartell leaves home and moves to Lincoln, Kansas, where he begins work in a drugstore. His employer is also president of the state pharmaceutical association, and over the next four years trains young Bartell in the pharmacy business.

1887 Bartell becomes a licensed pharmacist after completing a year's apprenticeship.

2711 S Jackson Street) in what today is known as the Leschi neighborhood of Seattle.

1890s In his early days at the pharmacy, Bartell compounds nearly all his prescriptions. Liquids are the most commonly used method to dispense medication, but Bartell also hand-rolls pills and

1898 Bartell opens Bartell's Owl Drugstore at 506 2nd Avenue. The "owl" comes from the all-night hours that a pharmacist is available to fill a prescription.

1900 Bartell names his business The Bartell Drug Company.

1900 Bartell sells the original Lake Washington Pharmacy to an associate,

January 23, 1904 The Bartell Drug Company formally incorporates.

October 1, 1904 Bartell opens a second store at 610 2nd Avenue in Seattle, which for the next ten years is known as both his main store and the Red Cross Annex.

October 18, 1905 Bartell marries Beatrice Shaffer. They live in a house built by

opens at 1416 2nd Avenue in the Shafer Building in December. The 2nd Avenue store is the first Bartell soda fountain to regularly serve hot meals.

1910 Bartell purchases the 2nd Avenue store (formerly the Raven Drugstore) with Bartell Drug Company stock. This creates a minority-shareholder interest in the company.

c. 1913 Bartell opens a candy factory at 1906 Boren Avenue. The candy

Summer 1887 Bartell moves to Seattle. Over the next several years he works a series of odd jobs, and briefly lives on Whidbey Island.

Late March 1890 George Bartell begins part-time work at the Lake Washington Pharmacy in Seattle, and in June he is hired full time. Two weeks later, he purchases the pharmacy with $3,000 borrowed from its owner, Dr. Horace Hall. The pharmacy is located at 2911 Jackson Street (later renumbered

powders and occasionally prescribes suppositories. He makes fluid extracts, tinctures, infusions, and mustard plasters. He also sells patent medicines, spices, and horse medicines.

1897–1898 Bartell leaves the Lake Washington Pharmacy and travels to the Yukon to prospect for gold. After factoring in expenses, he breaks even, but returns to Seattle in 1898 with an ambitious plan to open several drugstores in downtown Seattle.

Bert Weed, and focuses his operations at his location on 2nd Avenue.

1901–1904 Bartell battles the "Seattle Drug Trust" in an acrimonious rivalry brought on by his refusal to raise prices to match those charged by the trust. He runs a series of more than one hundred ads in *The Seattle Times* between 1901 and 1904 listing his bargain prices and decrying the evils of the trust.

Spring 1902 Bartell opens one of Seattle's first soda fountains at the Owl Drugstore.

her father, Fisk Shaffer, at 1517 11th Avenue W in the Queen Anne neighborhood of Seattle, and have two children, Amy and George Jr., but divorce about 1920.

October 1908 Bartell opens a third store at 1435 1st Avenue in Seattle, located on the southwest corner of 1st Avenue and Pike Street next to Pike Place Market. The store remains open until September 1961.

1910 Two more Bartell stores open during 1910. Store No. 4 opens at 5344 Ballard Avenue in Ballard in May, and Store No. 5

FROM LEFT: *George Bartell in the early 1890s, soon after he became owner of the Lake Washington Pharmacy.*

A circa-1900 pill roller on display at Bartell's corporate office in Seattle, December 2009.

Another view of Bartell's Denny Building store, 1910s.

Scales, weights, and medicines from the early twentieth century on display at Bartell's corporate office in Seattle, December 2009.

Bartell's peanut brittle on display.

factory will remain open for approximately twenty-five years. By 1930, Bartell's will produce and sell a ton of candy daily.

1914 Bartell's headquarters is moved to 1906 Boren Avenue. This building will later also house the company's medical laboratory and warehouse.

October 20, 1916 George Bartell Jr. is born in Seattle.

1917 Bartell Drugs opens a photo laboratory at the company headquarters. The photo lab operates until

1922 George Bartell forms the G. Henbart Company, a commercial real estate investment company. Over the years, the Henbart Company purchases property that it subsequently leases to Bartell Drugs for its stores; later, the two companies merge.

December 2, 1922 Bartell Drugs acquires a new store at 1501 2nd Avenue (the northwest corner of 2nd Avenue and Pike Street) from Louis F. Swift, another early chain drugstore owner in Seattle. This store

October 15, 1925 Bartell, who is in New York on unrelated business, meets with representatives of the United Drug Company to discuss their offer. United Drug increases the offer to approximately $1 million.

November 12, 1925 Bartell meets with his executive board and store managers and puts the buyout offer to a vote. The offer is unanimously rejected. Bartell also asks his 9-year-old son,

May 1928 Bartell Drugs moves its office next door to a new building at 1916 Boren Avenue. This location will remain the company's headquarters until April 1985.

1929 The decade of the 1920s ends with ten new Bartell drugstores having been added in Seattle during the preceding ten years, and brings the total of active Bartell Drugs locations to fifteen.

FROM LEFT: *A 1920s picture of Bartell and business associates; at least some of the men pictured were managers of his stores. Bartell's long-time associate P.G. Power is behind Bartell and immediately to his right.*
George Bartell in the 1920s.
George Bartell Jr. and Beatrice Bartell on a road trip to the mountains, ca. 1924.
Workers in Bartell's photo lab, April 1930.
A Bartell's soda fountain in the 1930s.

the late 1950s, and by the 1930s is capable of developing and returning prints to its store locations in Seattle within a five-hour period.

1920s By the 1920s, pharmacists gradually are starting to use more drugs purchased from manufacturers instead of compounding their own prescriptions. However, it will be several decades before manufacturer-produced drugs make up a majority of prescriptions dispensed by a pharmacist.

is probably the first Bartell location to have a second-floor tearoom in addition to a soda fountain.

September 2, 1925 Bartell's opens its tenth store at 1820 N 45th Street in Wallingford.

September 1925 Liggett's Inc., a subsidiary of the United Drug Company, one of the largest pharmacy chains in the world, offers to purchase Bartell's ten stores for an undisclosed sum.

George Bartell Jr., for his advice; he likewise suggests the offer be declined.

September 1, 1926 Bartell Drugs opens its eleventh store at 4342 University Way NE in Seattle's University District. The store moves next door in the 1940s, and then expands in 1986 to incorporate its original space. Of the more than one hundred locations where the company has had a store since 1890, this location stands out as the longest occupied by a Bartell Drugs.

1934 Bartell Drugs opens Store No. 20 at 620 Broadway Avenue N in Seattle.

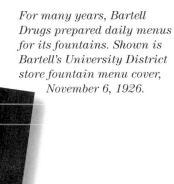

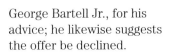

For many years, Bartell Drugs prepared daily menus for its fountains. Shown is Bartell's University District store fountain menu cover, November 6, 1926.

July 1935 George Bartell leases a site at 401 Pine Street in downtown Seattle, where a new store is built later that year. Located where Westlake Park is today, the store becomes known as the triangle store because of the shape of the building. It also becomes one of Bartell's flagship stores, and remains open for nearly fifty years.

August 5, 1935 At the request of George Bartell Sr., George Bartell Jr. drops out of college after

one year at the University of Washington and begins working for the Bartell Drug Company.

1937 Congress passes the Miller-Tydings Fair Trade Act, which gives manufacturers the ability to control the minimum retail price of various products purchased from the manufacturer for resale. The effects of the law adversely affect Bartell's business in the 1940s and 1950s.

1938 George Bartell Jr. is put in charge of supervising the design, construction, and remodeling of the company's stores.

September 1, 1938 Bartell Drugs moves Store No. 12 to a new location at 4554 California Avenue in West Seattle,

which George Bartell Jr. helped design. He will be involved in the layout work of many of the company's stores for most of the next fifty years.

September 27, 1939 George Bartell Jr. becomes president of the Bartell Drug Company. George Bartell Sr. becomes secretary of the company, but will remain active in store operations until his death in 1956.

1940 The Bartell Drug Company celebrates fifty years in business.

January 1940 The Bartell Drug Company and the G. Henbart Company are combined. Henbart becomes the parent company and Bartell

Drugs becomes a wholly owned subsidiary.

June 1940 Bartell Drugs opens its twenty-second store, located at 7804 Aurora Avenue N. Bartell's will add only one more store during the 1940s.

December 1941 The United States enters World War II. Among the effects: Bartell's, which is already progressive in hiring women, will hire even more

of them to fill positions formerly held by men who are in the war.

May 1942 George Bartell Jr. is drafted into the Army, and eventually is sent to Japan as part of the occupation force after the war. Although he remains president of the company, George Bartell Sr. essentially assumes the duties of president until the younger Bartell returns four years later.

March 1946 George Bartell Jr. is discharged from the Army and returns to Seattle and the Bartell Drug Company.

December 1, 1948 George Bartell Jr. marries Elizabeth "Betty" Bogue. They live their entire married lives in Seattle's Magnolia neighborhood and have three children: George D., Jean, and Robert.

May 16, 1951 Bartell Drugs opens a store in the Northgate Shopping Mall in Seattle. Opened in 1950, Northgate is the nation's first regional shopping center defined as a mall.

September 7, 1951 George D. Bartell is born in Seattle.

March 17, 1953 Jean Bartell is born in Seattle.

December 10, 1953 Bartell Drugs opens its first Eastside location in Bellevue, across the street from Bellevue Square. It's also Bartell's first self-service drugstore.

August 26, 1954 Robert Bartell is born in Seattle.

March 30, 1956 George Bartell dies at age 87.

THIS PAGE, TOP: *A Bartell photo lab envelope from the late 1930s.*

CENTER, FROM LEFT: *1930's streetcar with Bartell Drugs ad.*

ABOVE: *Bartell's Triangle store, 1937.*

BELOW: *Bartell's modern Mack Junior delivery truck in action in 1936.*

During World War II, Bartell Drugs participated in a drive to collect razors for the men fighting overseas.

A happy crowd rings in New Year's in Seattle and Bartell Drugs is there, 1950s.

it has twelve stores in operation.

October 10, 1961 Bartell hires Fred Damlos, former director of merchandising for Rexall Drugs in Los Angeles, as general manager of Bartell Drugs.

April–October 1962 The Century 21 Exposition, otherwise known as the Seattle World's Fair, is held. The southern terminus of the new monorail is next to the triangle store. Many celebrities (such as Elvis Presley and George Burns) who visit Seattle to see the fair also visit the triangle store.

September 1, 1964 Damlos resigns. Bartell again becomes president of the company. George Kanrich is hired as an administrative vice president, and Robert Thornberg is hired as operations manager.

February 19, 1965 Bartell Drugs terminates its contract with Kanrich and Thornberg. Val Storrs, store manager at the Bellevue No. 13 store, is promoted to operations manager. Gordon O'Reilly, store manager at the Ballard No. 4 store, is promoted

Summer 1968 George D. Bartell begins working for the company as a clerk-cashier in the triangle store in downtown Seattle.

1970 By 1970, compounded prescriptions make up only 1 percent of all prescriptions filled.

Summer 1971 Jean Bartell first works for the company as a retail clerk in the triangle store.

c. 1973 Bartell Drugs introduces electronic order transmission, enabling each store to write its own restocking orders.

1975 The Miller-Tydings Act is repealed, although many jurisdictions already have stopped enforcing it, recognizing the impracticalities of price-control laws.

April 1977 Bartell Drugs opens a store in Seattle's Magnolia neighborhood and names George D. Bartell manager. The store is the most successful new store opening for Bartell Drugs in more than twenty years, giving the company the confidence to expand more aggressively.

1956 Bartell Drugs now has twenty-three stores in operation, but over the next few years, it will close nearly half of them.

March 15, 1957 In one of his first significant acts as president after his father's death, George Bartell Jr. asks for the resignation of P. G. Power, vice president of Bartell Drugs.

August–October 1961 Between August 19 and October 14, the Bartell Drug Company closes six stores. By the end of 1961,

January 1963 Bartell Drugs implements a Senior Citizen's Prescription Plan, and offers all its customers over age 60 a 10 percent discount on prescriptions — the first drugstore in Seattle to offer such a discount.

June 6, 1963 George Bartell Jr. resigns as president of the Bartell Drug Company and is replaced by Damlos. Bartell becomes chairman of the board.

to merchandise manager. The company embarks on a "self-modernization" process that involves remodeling stores to update them and make them more uniform.

October 16, 1965 George Bartell Jr. purchases the shares of Bartell Drug Company stock owned by the company's minority shareholders.

October 1966 Bartell Drugs opens a store in Edmonds, its first in Snohomish County.

September 13, 1973 Bartell Drugs opens a store in Greenwood, increasing its store count to thirteen. This represents Bartell's first increase in stores in more than a decade. This store only operates for three months, but a more permanent thirteenth store follows in Renton in 1974.

1974 George D. Bartell becomes manager of Store No. 12 in West Seattle.

TOP LEFT, ABOVE: *George D. Bartell, ca. 1961.*

BELOW: *Jean Bartell, ca. 1961.*

CENTER, FROM LEFT:

Bartell's Store No. 19 on Roosevelt Way, February 27, 1956.

Bartell's White Center store, ca. 1960.

Bartell's Ballard store in the mid-1960s showing some of the changes brought by self-modernization.

1979 Bartell Drugs opens three new stores during the year, and ends the decade with seventeen stores in operation.

1979 Washington becomes one of the first states to allow pharmacists to participate in collaborative drug-therapy agreements with physicians. This enables pharmacists to prescribe medications, provide medication management, order laboratory tests, and give immunizations –services previously available only from physicians or nurse practitioners.

September 7, 1984 Bartell Drugs opens five new stores in a single day, all purchased from Shoppers Drug Mart, a Canadian chain. Four of the new locations are in Snohomish County.

April 19, 1985 After more than seventy years on Boren Avenue, Bartell moves its corporate office to 4930 3rd Avenue S in Seattle.

1986 Henbart and Bartell Drugs are fully merged, with Henbart becoming a division of Bartell Drugs.

1990 Bartell Drugs begins the decade with thirty-one stores. The company also enjoys a yearlong celebration of its centennial.

It's Bartell's first store in Pierce County. The store also offers a photo laboratory capable of developing pictures in one hour, marking the return of photo developing to Bartell stores after a hiatus of more than thirty years.

1993 Jean Bartell Barber joins Bartell Drugs. She handles most of the insurance operations for the company as well as many of its technology issues.

September 1, 1994 George D. Bartell becomes CEO of Bartell Drugs.

FROM LEFT: *Bartell's Magnolia store interior, 1977.*

The interior of Bartell's headquarters in 1985 harkened back to an earlier era.

ABOVE: *Jean Barber not long after her return to Seattle, August 1991.*

George D. Bartell, ca. 1992.

The Bartell and Barber families, ca. 1992.

Bob and Alina Bartell, 1990s.

1982 Bartell's last soda fountain, located at Store No. 14 at Northgate Mall, closes.

April 17, 1982 Jean Bartell marries Dave Barber. They have three children: Evelyn, Hugh, and Neal.

April 1984 The triangle store closes, and the building is later demolished to make way for the Westlake Center project.

June 1987 Bartell Drugs opens a large store in Seattle's University Village shopping center. The store is an immediate success, proving that the company can operate a large store successfully and returning it to a dominant position in the Seattle-area pharmacy market.

November 4, 1989 George Bartell marries June Erdman. They have two children: Claire and Mike.

January 12, 1990 Bartell Drugs moves its corporate office to 4727 Denver Avenue S in Seattle.

April 1, 1990 George H. Bartell Jr. steps down as president of the Bartell Drug Company and is succeeded by his son, George D. Bartell. George Bartell Jr. stays on as CEO and chairman of the board.

October 14, 1991 Bartell Drugs opens Store No. 39, located at 5500 Olympic Drive NW in Gig Harbor.

1995 Bartell Drugs introduces point-of-sale scanning in its stores, completing the project in about three years. This system enables the company to handle its inventory and sales far more efficiently than previously.

February 15, 1995 Bartell's opens Seattle's first modern twenty-four-hour drugstore at 600 1st Avenue N in Lower Queen Anne.

1997 George Bartell Sr. is inducted into the Junior Achievement Puget Sound Business Hall of Fame.

January 24, 2001 Bartell Drugs opens its fiftieth active store (known as Store No. 54) at 3601 6th Avenue in Tacoma. It's Bartell's first drugstore in Tacoma.

August 16, 2001 George D. Bartell succeeds his father as chairman of the board of Bartell Drugs. George Bartell Jr. becomes chairman emeritus.

December 2003 Bartell's introduces new self-service digital print centers in its stores, becoming one of the first major retailers

August 11, 2004 Bartell Drugs opens the Eastside's first twenty-four-hour drugstore near Crossroads Mall in Bellevue.

2006 Jean Barber becomes vice chairman and treasurer of Bartell Drugs.

October 15, 2012 Bartell Drugs moves its corporate office to 4025 Delridge Way SW in West Seattle.

2013 Bartell Drugs and Henbart become wholly owned subsidiaries of a new parent company, B. Alliance Holdings, Inc.

LEFT TO RIGHT: *Westlake Park in 2012, on the spot where Bartell's triangle store stood from 1935 until 1984.*
ABOVE: *Jean Bartell Barber, ca. 2009.*
George Bartell Jr., 1970s.
Bartell and Barber family outing, summer 2010.
BELOW: *George D. Bartell and son Mike cutting the ribbon at the grand opening of Bartell's Lake Serene store on July 21, 2009.*

1997 Jean Barber becomes chief financial officer of Bartell Drugs.

May 1998 Bartell Drugs inaugurates its first website.

January 1, 1999 Robert Bartell sells his shares in the Bartell Drug Company.

January 1, 2000 The Bartell Drug Company begins the new millennium with forty-five stores and more than thirteen hundred employees.

in Puget Sound to offer immediate on-site, self-service processing of prints from digital images.

July 12, 2004 The Bartell Drug Company is awarded the Washington State Century Corporation Award by Secretary of State Sam Reed. Bartell Drugs is one of only forty-three businesses remaining from the eight hundred incorporated in Washington in the year 1904.

January 21, 2009 George Bartell Jr. dies at age 92 in Mesa, Arizona. Bartell's now has fifty-four stores in operation in the greater Puget Sound region.

December 2009 Bartell's ends the first decade of the twenty-first century with fifty-seven stores in operation and approximately seventeen hundred full-time and part-time employees.

Afterword

The fourth generation, FROM LEFT: FRONT: *Evelyn Barber and Claire Bartell*; REAR: *Hugh Barber, Mike Bartell, Neal Barber, May 2014.*

The history of Bartell Drugs has shown that some things never go out of style, like treating our customers according to the Golden Rule, and like neighbors. We hope that Bartell's will continue to be a place that families rely on through the generations ahead — just as it has been since 1890.

We've grown up hearing stories about our great-grandfather George Sr., and we remember our grandfather George Jr. At the core of these stories are the values that our family has emphasized.

As the family's fourth and youngest generation—we range in age from high school to graduate school—we are very proud of the family legacy and plan to demonstrate the values going forward. We support finding new ways to make our customers' lives healthier and happier, just as our great-grandfather and our grandfather did, and as our parents continue to do today.

Our parents — George and June Bartell, and Jean and Dave Barber —continue to show us how things are done, and we plan to follow in their footsteps. Bartell Drugs is the oldest family-run drugstore chain in the country. We want to keep it that way. And, like every generation before us, we hope to build on our family's legacy and make it even stronger.

Claire Bartell

Evelyn Barber

Neal Barber

Mike Bartell

Hugh Barber

A Note on Sources

Most large and well-established companies that are more than a century old have historical records, and Bartell Drugs is no exception. It has several informal, unpublished company histories written by different family members and others over the years. These histories – particularly one titled "The First 100 Years" – served as the book's foundation, and helped provide a template for the rest of the story. Bartell's has more archival information consisting of various newspaper and magazine articles, company newsletters, internal bulletins, press releases, and a 1997 video about its history, and it supplied a wealth of information about Bartell Drugs and some of the personalities who worked there.

The Seattle Times searchable database on the Seattle Public Library's website was a godsend. Not only did *Times* reporters cover Bartell Drugs over the years, but Bartell employees also occasionally wrote articles about the company for the paper, such as the March 1950 series that gave a vivid description of nearly all of the company's operations as it celebrated its sixtieth birthday. Back issues of the *Seattle Post-Intelligencer* were also helpful, and even the long-defunct *Seattle Star* surprised with a 1930 Leo Lassen interview of George Bartell that provided a nice snapshot of Bartell in his prime.

Other local publications also played a role in the research. The *Puget Sound Business Journal* and the *Seattle Shopping News* (a shopping paper that operated between the 1920s and the 1970s) were two; articles from the national publication *Chain Drug Review* also contributed to the book.

Websites yielded more information. AllBusiness.com provided articles about the company's last ten to fifteen years. Ancestry.com furnished census records that were helpful in helping piece together personal information about the Bartells in the early twentieth century. The Washington State Digital Archives website likewise uncovered useful tidbits of personal histories and even a surprise or two, like George Bartell's first marriage, to Mary Heaney. And articles on HistoryLink.org, the free online encyclopedia of Washington State history, supplied background information about Seattle and its environs that helped put the story in context.

Two books provided background detail about the general history of pharmacy: The 1940 publication *History of Pharmacy* by Edward Kremers and George Urdang, and *Pharmacy: An Illustrated History*, written by David Cowen and William Hefland fifty years later. A 1929 article in the *Washington Historical Quarterly* contributed valuable information about the first pharmacies in Washington Territory, while Frederic Grant's 1891 *History of Seattle, Washington* supplied information about the first pharmacies in Seattle. Finally, a number of in-person and telephone interviews of current and former Bartell personnel played a big role in the book's development; without these first-hand accounts, the story would have been far less complete.

Photo Credits

Front cover

George Bartell, May 1890. Courtesy Bartell Drugs (1890.01.8).

A depiction of Bartell's Lake Washington Pharmacy in the early 1890s. Courtesy Marie McCaffrey.

Back cover

George Bartell, 1890. Courtesy Bartell Drugs (1890.01.9).

George Bartell Jr., 1970s. Courtesy Bartell Drugs (1966.01.2).

Jean Bartell Barber and George D. Bartell, May 2014. Courtesy Bartell Drugs.

Front flap

Pharmacist Colin McCord prepares a prescription, 1910s. (Courtesy Bartell Drugs)

Back flap

A Bartell's soda fountain in the 1930s. Courtesy Bartell Drugs.

Title page

George Bartell, May 1890. Courtesy Bartell Drugs (1890.01.8).

p. 4

Frank A. Blethen, 2012. Courtesy *The Seattle Times.*

p. 6

Looking north on 2nd Avenue from Yesler Way, ca. 1905. Bartell's Owl Drugstore is visible on the extreme right. Courtesy Bartell Drugs (1905.01.1).

p. 8

The Lake Washington Pharmacy at 2911 Jackson Street in the early 1890s. Courtesy Bartell Drugs (1890.01.5).

p. 9

Augustus Bartell (left), Mary Ann Bartell. Courtesy Bartell Drugs.

p. 10

A family sketch of George Bartell as a teenager in the 1880s. Courtesy Bartell Drugs.

Corner 2nd Avenue and Cherry Street looking south in June 1889, shortly after the Great Seattle Fire. Note all of the temporary tents in the pictures that were set up for businesses to continue operating. Courtesy Bartell Drugs (1889.01.3).

A locomotive near the new Stampede Pass Tunnel, ca. 1888. Courtesy Museum of History and Industry (1986.17.14).

p. 11

Seattle's first streetcar, September 1884. Courtesy Museum of History and Industry (2002.3.439).

p. 12

Emmet Case (left) and Edward Lawler (right) in front of the Lake Washington Pharmacy, August 1897. Lawler worked for George Bartell between 1895 and 1897, and decades later sent this picture to George Bartell Jr. with a note that "I thought it might be of interest to you." Courtesy Bartell Drugs (1897.01.1).

p. 13

George Bartell, 1890. Courtesy Bartell Drugs (1890.01.9).

George Bartell's first listing as a druggist in the Seattle Polk City Directory, 1890. Courtesy Bartell Drugs.

p. 14

The Kellogg and Brother drugstore on Yesler Way shortly after its 1865 opening. Courtesy University of Washington Libraries, Special Collections (UW 2245).

Gardner Kellogg, an early druggist in Seattle, about the time he became Seattle's first fire chief in 1889. Courtesy Museum of History and Industry (shs 111).

p. 15

A view inside a nineteenth-century drugstore. Courtesy Bartell Drugs (1890.01.6).

Peruna ad, ca. 1900. (Courtesy American Antiquities.com).

p. 16

A completed prescription blank from June 1890 by Dr. James Shannon; the Lake Washington Pharmacy is advertised on the back. Courtesy Bartell Drugs.

p. 17

A Bartell Drugs quinine capsule box from the early 1900s. Note the emphasis on service, even in those early days. Courtesy Bartell Drugs.

A view of the southeast corner of 2nd Avenue and James Street shortly after George Bartell opened his Owl Drugstore down the block in 1898. The store is just visible on the right. Courtesy Museum of History and Industry, Anders B. Wilse Collection (1988.33.222).

p. 18

Bartell's Owl Drugstore, ca. 1907. Courtesy Bartell Drugs (1907.01.2).

p. 19

Forest's Juniper Tar Compound, a patent medicine sold by Bartell Drugs in the early 1900s for nasal congestion and throat irritation. Its 22 percent alcohol content also made it useful as a disinfectant for small cuts and burns. Courtesy Bartell Drugs (1900.04.80).

p. 20

A Bartell antitrust ad in The Seattle Times *in 1902 kept the "trust druggists" in an unwelcome spotlight.* Courtesy *The Seattle Times.*

p. 21

An undated photo of the Bartell family home at 1517 11th Avenue W in Seattle. Courtesy Bartell Drugs (1900.01.4).

Beatrice Shaffer as a young woman, ca. 1900. Courtesy Bartell Drugs (1890.01.12).

p. 22

A Bartell antitrust ad in The Seattle Times, *December 3, 1901.* Courtesy *The Seattle Times.*

p. 23

Amy and George Bartell Jr. in 1917. Courtesy Bartell Drugs (1917.01.1).

A Bartell ad in The Seattle Times *on September 30, 1904, announced the opening of the Red Cross Annex store.* Courtesy *The Seattle Times.*

p. 24

A view of Pike Place Market, ca. 1912. The sign for Bartell's Store No. 3 is just visible on the left. Courtesy Museum of History and Industry, PEMCO Webster and Stevens Collection (1983.10.10020).

Bartell cough syrup bottle, ca. 1910. Courtesy Bartell Drugs.

p. 25

Looking north on 2nd Avenue from James Street, ca. 1908. Bartell's Red Cross Annex store is in the lower right. Courtesy Museum of History and Industry, PEMCO Webster and Stevens Collection (1983.10.7495.1).

p. 26

George Bartell (second from left) and friends show off their catch after a fishing trip, 1930s. Courtesy Bartell Drugs (1930.01.227).

A colorized photo of George Bartell (second from left) on the links at Seattle's Olympic Golf Club in 1929. Courtesy Bartell Drugs (1929.01.15).

p. 27
Bartell's Denny Building store, ca. 1918. Courtesy Bartell Drugs (1918.01.1).

An early view of Bartell Drugs' medicinal lab, believed to date from the 1910s. Courtesy Bartell Drugs (1915.01.2).

A circa 1905 medicine label for Salvosine, a formula used to treat "catarrh" (congestion), alerted the user that it contained 16 percent alcohol. Courtesy Bartell Drugs.

p. 28
In 1913, Bartell's moved its Ballard store across the street to 5349 Ballard Avenue, where it remained until 1929. Courtesy Bartell Drugs (1929.01.2).

An interior view of Bartell's first Ballard store at 5344 Ballard Avenue shortly after its 1910 opening. Courtesy Bartell Drugs (1911.01.2).

p. 29
Bartell's original headquarters and its Store No. 1 at 1906 Boren Avenue, ca. 1927. Courtesy Bartell Drugs (1930.01.1).

Pharmacist Colin McCord prepares a prescription, 1910s. Courtesy Bartell Drugs.

p. 30
George Bartell in the early 1900s. Courtesy Bartell Drugs (1895.01.1)

A Lydia Pinkham's vegetable compound ad from World War I in 1917-1918. Courtesy Alltop.com.

p. 31
Various bottles from Bartell's medicinal lab dating from the first half of the twentieth century. Courtesy Bartell Drugs.

A Bartell ad in The Seattle Times *late in 1919 offered Kodaks, clocks, percolators, and more.* Courtesy *The Seattle Times.*

p. 32
An Ovaltine display at one of Bartell's stores in the 1930s. These displays were common in Bartell

stores during these years. Courtesy Bartell Drugs (1930.01.66).

p. 33
Bartell delivery truck, 1928. Courtesy Bartell Drugs.

p. 34
The Bartell candy factory at 1906 Boren, ca. 1922. Courtesy Bartell Drugs (1925.01.2).

Two workers proudly pose in the candy kitchen, ca. 1930. Courtesy Bartell Drugs (1930.01.16).

p. 35
Cooking candy in the candy factory, ca. 1930. Courtesy Bartell Drugs (1930.01.15).

Two Bartell workers coating chocolate candies in the candy kitchen, ca. 1930. Courtesy Bartell Drugs (1930.01.10).

p. 36
A Bartell ad for treats from its candy factory in The Seattle Times, *March 20, 1930.* Courtesy *The Seattle Times.*

p. 37
Bartell store window display for licorice candy, ca.1930. Courtesy Bartell Drugs (1930.01.466).

p. 38
George Bartell, pictured in the middle, on a National Association of Chain Drug Stores cruise in 1933. Courtesy Bartell Drugs (1933.01.1).

Looking north on 2nd Avenue from Yesler Way in 1902.G.O. Guy Drugs, established in Seattle in 1888, dominates the left half of the picture.Bartell's Owl Drugstore, not visible in the picture, is across 2nd Avenue on the right. Courtesy University of Washington Libraries, Special Collections (UW 23711).

p. 39
Bartell window display, ca. 1930. Courtesy Bartell Drugs (1930.01.217).

p. 40
Bartell's French Cleaner. Courtesy Bartell Drugs.

A model displays the Olympic Oscillator in a "live" window display at Bartell's Store No. 9 on

the corner of 2nd Avenue and Pike Street, November 22, 1929. Courtesy Bartell Drugs (1929.01.25).

p. 41
A Bartell Drugs ad in the Seattle Shopping News *from 1936.* Courtesy Bartell Drugs.

Bartell Drugs held a special dinner on November 4, 1938, to honor its Asian employees. George Bartell is seated in the middle, while George Bartell Jr. appears second from the right. Courtesy Bartell Drugs (1938.01.15).

p. 42
A nattily attired and confident Bartell photo courier with a load in front of a downtown Bartell store, 1930s. Courtesy Bartell Drugs (1940.01.50).

p. 43
The Bartell family in 1932. Seated in front are George Bartell Sr., daughter Amy Bartell Meakin, and Beatrice Bartell; seated above are Harry Meakin and George Bartell Jr. Courtesy Bartell Drugs (1932.01.11).

Bartell photo receipt, 1935. Courtesy Bartell Drugs.

p. 44
A prescription label on the back of a pint of legal medicinal whiskey, sold at Bartell's Ballard store on July 14, 1933. Courtesy Bartell Drugs.

p. 45
Bartell's triangle store as seen from Westlake Avenue, 1937. Courtesy Bartell Drugs (1940.01.45).

Bartell's triangle store tearoom. Courtesy Bartell Drugs (1984.01.15).

The soda fountain at Bartell's triangle store, 1930s. Courtesy Bartell Drugs (1935.01.14).

p. 46
George Bartell Jr., ca. 1936. Courtesy Bartell Drugs (1940.01.52).

p. 47
Bartell's Store No. 7 — Southwest corner of 5th Avenue and Pike

Street, 1922. Courtesy Bartell Drugs (1935.01.1).

Bartell's Store No. 11 — University Way in Seattle's University District, 1929. Courtesy Bartell Drugs (1937.01.3).

Bartell's Store No. 8 — Southwest corner of 1st Avenue and Yesler Way, 1921. Courtesy Bartell Drugs (1924.01.3).

Bartell's Store No. 12 — Seattle's Orpheum Theater, 1928. Courtesy Bartell Drugs (1928.01.1).

p. 48
Bartell's Store No. 22 on Aurora Avenue shortly after its June 1940 opening. Courtesy Bartell Drugs (1950.01.20).

p. 49
Bartell's 1940 gift catalog cover. Courtesy Bartell Drugs.

p. 50
Bartell's tailored its window displays to the times, as this display featured during World War II shows, ca. 1942. Courtesy Bartell Drugs (1941.01.15).

p. 51
George Bartell Jr. during his Army years, ca. 1944. Courtesy Bartell Drugs (1936.01.4).

George Bartell Jr., in the middle, taking a break in the South Pacific, ca. 1945. Courtesy Bartell Drugs (1945.01.2).

p. 52
A look inside Store No. 19 on Roosevelt Way in the 1950s. Manager William Pappe is smiling at the camera. Courtesy Bartell Drugs.

A page from a 1940 Bartell gift catalog offered a broad range of gifts. Courtesy Bartell Drugs.

p. 53
George Bartell at his country home near Meadowdale in Snohomish County, 1940s. Courtesy Bartell Drugs (1938.01.9).

Betty and George Bartell Jr. on their wedding day, Seattle, December 1, 1948. Courtesy Bartell Drugs.

p. 54

Bartell's sixtieth anniversary was prominently featured in an article in The Seattle Times *on March 26, 1950. Courtesy* The Seattle Times.

Advertising manager Ed Arbow designs an ad commemorating Bartell's sixtieth anniversary inside Bartell's sign shop, 1950. Courtesy Bartell Drugs (1950.01.109).

Supervisor Eve Comstock (right) training members of Bartell's cosmetics department, 1950. Courtesy Bartell Drugs (1950.01.56).

p. 55

George Bartell, Amy Bartell Meakin, and George Bartell Jr. at a Bartell Drugs manager's dinner commemorating the company's sixtieth anniversary, 1950. Courtesy Bartell Drugs (1950.01.86).

p. 56

Celebrating the opening of Bartell's new Northgate store with a square dance in the adjacent parking lot, May 1951. Courtesy Bartell Drugs (1950.01.34).

Northgate store opening in May 1951. Courtesy Bartell Drugs (1950.01.4).

A two-page ad in The Seattle Times *on May 15, 1951, celebrated the opening of Bartell's new store at Seattle's Northgate Mall.* Courtesy The Seattle Times.

A rainy-day shot of the entrance to Bartell Drugs' Northgate store not long after its opening in May 1951. Courtesy Bartell Drugs (1950.01.36).

p. 57

A manager's meeting at Store No. 8 about 1950. General Merchandise Manager Harry Morrison is standing. Seated to his left are (from left) George Bartell Jr., P.G. Power, and George Bartell Sr. Courtesy Bartell Drugs (1950.01.112).

p. 58

Bartell's University District store dining area, ca. 1948. Courtesy Bartell Drugs (1949.01.1).

"Bartell soda fountain girls" (and a short-order cook behind them) at the Northgate soda fountain, ca. 1955. Courtesy Bartell Drugs (1955.01.35).

p. 59

Soda fountain patrons both ignore and stare down the photographer at Bartell's Store No. 23 on Mercer Street in February 1948. Courtesy Bartell Drugs (1946.01.5).

Bartell's triangle store tearoom menu cover and inside page, 1952. Courtesy Bartell Drugs.

p. 60

George Bartell, ca. late 1940s. Courtesy Bartell Drugs (1948.01.39).

A photo montage of George Bartell Jr. taken shortly after his return to Bartell Drugs in 1946. Courtesy Bartell Drugs, Image no. (1946.01.19).

p. 61

Bartell's original Bellevue store on what is today Bellevue Way, 1950s. Courtesy Bartell Drugs (1962.01.5).

A look inside Bartell's first Eastside store, Bellevue, mid-1950s. Courtesy Bartell Drugs (1962.01.2).

Bartell's Renton store in the early 1960s. Courtesy Bartell Drugs (1960.01.9).

p. 62

A view of the monorail entrance and Bartell's triangle store, 1963. Courtesy Seattle Municipal Archives (30682).

p. 63

An article in The Seattle Times *three weeks after George Bartell's 1956 death reassured readers that the "Policy at Bartell's (is) Unchanged."* Courtesy The Seattle Times.

p. 64

Bartell's Store No. 9 in Greenwood, 1959. The store was at this location from 1958 until 2013, when it moved next door. Courtesy Bartell Drugs (1958.01.1).

George Bartell Jr. and P.G. Power at Bartell sixty-sixth anniversary dinner, April 1956. Courtesy Bartell Drugs (1956.01.4).

p. 65

Bartell's new Burien store, August 1957. Courtesy Bartell Drugs (1957.01.1).

Bartell's new White Center store on opening day, December 8, 1959. Courtesy Bartell Drugs (1959.01.1).

pp. 66-67

A sketch of a proposal for the Lake Union Building, 1969. Courtesy Bartell Drugs.

p. 68

George Bartell Jr. and Fred Damlos at the opening of the new Bellevue store, 1962. Courtesy Bartell Drugs (1963.01.1).

The Bartell family in 1964. Robert, Betty, and Jean Bartell are in front; George Bartell Jr. and George D. Bartell stand behind. Courtesy Bartell Drugs.

p. 69

In August 1963 Bartell Drugs held a drawing for a free 1963 Rambler to celebrate its Bellevue store opening. Shown are the happy winners. Courtesy Bartell Drugs (1963.01.7).

p. 70

Seattle World's Fair pennant. Courtesy Paula Becker.

p. 71

Booklet detailing contract terms between members of the Seattle-King County Pharmaceutical Society and the Greater Seattle Retail Drug Association (which included Bartell Drugs) and the Pharmacists and Retail Drugstore Employees Union, 1968-1970. Courtesy Bartell Drugs.

p. 72

J.L. Terrill, regional manager for the pharmaceutical company Squibb, presents pharmacist Lionel Gilmore (left) and George Bartell Jr. (right) with a plaque commemorating Bartell Drugs filling eight million prescriptions in the Seattle area since 1890, March 1962. Courtesy Bartell Drugs (1962.01.11).

Bartell pharmacist Lionel Gilmour beams as he reads about Bartell's

new Senior Citizens Prescription Plan in The Seattle Times, *1963.* Courtesy Bartell Drugs (1962.01.10).

p. 73

P.G. Power, 1950. Courtesy Bartell Drugs (1950.01.98).

p. 74

Cover of Bartell Drugs breakfast menu, 1969. Courtesy Bartell Drugs.

p. 75

A relaxed George Bartell Jr. confidently greets a new decade in 1970. Courtesy Bartell Drugs (1970.01.8).

p. 76

An undated Bartell publication, likely from the 1960s, explained how Bartell's was moving forward with what later became known as "self-modernization." Courtesy Bartell Drugs (1966.02.01).

p. 77

A Bartell ad in The Seattle Times *featured a 44 cent sale on April 26, 1966.* Courtesy The Seattle Times.

p. 78

A Seattle Times *article on October 23, 1966, announced the opening of Parker Plaza in Edmonds, and with it Bartell's first store outside of King County.* Courtesy The Seattle Times.

p. 79

Gordon O' Reilly, ca. 1965. Courtesy Bartell Drugs (1955.01.30).

Gordon O' Reilly at Bartell headquarters, 1990. Courtesy Bartell Drugs (1990.01.140).

p. 80

George, Jean, and Robert Bartell, ca. 1975. Courtesy Bartell Drugs (1975.01.6)

p. 81

Bartell's West Seattle store before self-modernization, mid-1970s. Courtesy Bartell Drugs (1950.01.31).

Bartell's West Seattle store after self-modernization, late 1970s. Courtesy Bartell Drugs (1970.01.3).

p. 82

Val Storrs, ca. 1965. Courtesy Bartell Drugs (1961.01.8).

p. 83

George D. Bartell at Bartell's new Magnolia store, 1977. Courtesy Bartell Drugs (1977.01.13).

p. 85

Bartell's Ballard store in the 1970s. Courtesy Bartell Drugs (1975.01.1).

Bartell's Store No. 18 in Kirkland, 1979. Courtesy Bartell Drugs (1979.01.07).

Grand opening of Bartell's Magnolia store, April 1977. Courtesy Bartell Drugs (1977.01.6).

Bartell's Magnolia store interior, 1977. Courtesy Bartell Drugs (1977.01.12).

Sanford "Sandy" Barnes, ca. 1963. Courtesy Bartell Drugs (1963.01.6).

p. 86

Flyover picture of Bartell employees forming "100" in celebration of Bartell's 100th anniversary, 1990. Courtesy Bartell Drugs (1990.01.159).

p. 87

Bartell ad announcing the end of Pay'n Save and inviting its shoppers to Bartell Drugs, 1992. Courtesy Bartell Drugs (1992.01.4).

p. 89

An article in The Seattle Times *on June 25, 1987, discussed Pay'n Save's difficulties and Bartell's expansion.* Courtesy *The Seattle Times.*

Bartell Drugs 1916 Boren Avenue headquarters, 1985. Bartell Drugs moved its headquarters shortly after this picture was taken, after having been on this Boren Avenue block for more than seventy years. Courtesy Bartell Drugs (1985.01.19).

p. 90

Jean Bartell and David Barber on their wedding day, April 17, 1982. Courtesy Jean Barber.

Jean Bartell Barber in Charlotte, NC, ca. 1982. Courtesy Jean Barber.

p. 91

George D. and June Bartell on their wedding day, November 4, 1989. Courtesy George D. Bartell.

George Bartell Jr. and George D. Bartell, 1990. Courtesy Bartell Drugs.

p. 92

Bartell's Store No. 2 at its new location in the Crossroads Shopping Center in Bellevue, 1981. Courtesy Bartell Drugs (1981.01.18).

One of the five new stores purchased by Bartell Drugs from Shoppers Drug Mart in 1984: Store No. 25 at Silverlake in Everett. Courtesy Bartell Drugs (1984.01.35).

Another Bartell purchase from Shoppers: Store No. 27 in Lynnwood. Courtesy Bartell Drugs. (1984.01.19).

p. 93

Bartell's centennial bus, 1990. This Seattle Metro bus, sponsored by Bartell Drugs to promote its centennial, was hard to miss on the streets of downtown Seattle. Courtesy Bartell Drugs (1990.01.94).

p. 95

A Halloween candy display store at Bartell's Auburn store in 1995 demonstrates the change during the twentieth century from the sale of freshly-baked candy at Bartell Drugs to processed candy. Courtesy Bartell Drugs (1995.01.13).

Bartell's University Village store, 1990. Courtesy Bartell Drugs (1990.01.17).

Bartell Drugs opened its first store in Pierce County when it cut the ribbon for its Gig Harbor store on October 14, 1991. George D. Bartell is on the far right. Courtesy Bartell Drugs. (1991.01.1).

Bartell's grand opening of its Marysville store, October 13, 1999. George Bartell Jr. is directly behind the scissor blades, while George D. Bartell is on the far right. Courtesy Bartell Drugs.

p. 96

George Bartell Jr. golfing at a young age, ca. 1921. Courtesy Bartell Drugs (1919.01.3).

p. 97

George Bartell Jr. holding a "special edition — Bartell extra" section that appeared in The Seattle Times *during Bartell's 1990 centennial.* Courtesy Bartell Drugs (1990.01.121).

George Bartell Jr. (shown on the far right) golfing with friends in Yakima, 1977. Courtesy Bartell Drugs (1977.01.9).

George and Betty Bartell at George D. Bartell's wedding, November 4, 1989. Courtesy Jean Barber.

p. 98

A Bartell Drugs mural on a West Seattle wall, November 22, 2002. Courtesy Seattle Municipal Archives (134884).

p. 99

George D. Bartell and Jean Bartell Barber receiving the Best in the Northwest Washington Family Business Award, November 2006. Courtesy Bartell Drugs.

p. 101

Bartell Century Corporation award, 2004. Courtesy Bartell Drugs.

p. 102

Jean Barber, George Bartell Jr., and George D. Bartell, ca. 2003. Courtesy Bartell Drugs.

Bartell Store No. 61 at 4th Avenue and Madison Street, ca. 2010. Courtesy Bartell Drugs.

p. 103

Val Storrs congratulates a store employee at the opening of Store No. 54 in Tacoma on January 24, 2001. Courtesy Bartell Drugs.

Well-known clown J.P. Patches was on hand to celebrate Bartell's opening of its Stanwood store in November 2005. Courtesy Bartell Drugs.

p. 104

Bartell's University District store in the lower right, 1938. The store moved next door to the corner in the 1940s, and in 1986, the store expanded to include its original location. Courtesy Seattle Municipal Archives (18539).

A shot from the late 1940s showing the University District store in its present location. Courtesy University of Washington Libraries, Special Collections (SEA 3619).

Bartell's University District store, ca. 1975. Courtesy Bartell Drugs (1970.01.7.).

Bartell's University District store, June 14, 2002. Courtesy Seattle Municipal Archives (130471).

p. 106

Bartell's digital photo lab in its Sammamish store before remodel, May 2012. Courtesy Phil Dougherty.

Bartell's digital photo lab in its Sammamish store after remodel, August 2013. Courtesy Phil Dougherty.

Interior of Bartell's Sammamish store before remodel, May 2012. Courtesy Phil Dougherty.

Interior of Bartell's Sammamish store after remodel, August 2013. Courtesy Phil Dougherty.

p. 107

Every year Bartell Drugs teams up with an area radio station to help collect teddy bears, which are then distributed to emergency responders to help calm a scared child in a crisis. Pictured here is the 2013 "teddy bear patrol" consisting of members of the Des Moines police and radio station WARM 106.9, March 2013. Courtesy Bartell Drugs.

p. 108

The Barber family at son Hugh's graduation from Rhodes college, June 2011. From left: Neal, Jean, Hugh, Evelyn, and Dave Barber. Courtesy Jean Barber.

The George D. Bartell family at the opening of Bartell's Lake Union store, August 6, 2013. From left: Claire, Mike, June and George D. Bartell. Courtesy George D. Bartell.

p. 109

The Bartell Drugs warehouse, 2012. Courtesy Bartell Drugs.

"Bart" — a nickname for "Bartell's historic delivery truck"— often appears at grand openings, such as the one shown here near Lake Serene in Lynnwood on July 21, 2009. Courtesy Bartell Drugs.

p. 110

Bartell's Store No. 9 — Greenwood, 2010. Courtesy Bartell Drugs.

Bartell's Headquarters — West Seattle, 2014. Courtesy Bartell Drugs.

Bartell's Store No. 31 — University Village, 2010. Courtesy Bartell Drugs.

Bartell's Store No. 39 — Gig Harbor, 2013. Courtesy Bartell Drugs.

p. 111

Bartell's Store No. 66 — Lake City, 2008. Courtesy Bartell Drugs.

Bartell's Store No. 29 — Sammamish, 2014. Courtesy Bartell Drugs.

Bartell's Store No. 58 — Edmonds, 2003. Courtesy Bartell Drugs.

p. 112

George Bartell in the early 1890s, soon after he became owner of the Lake Washington Pharmacy. Courtesy Bartell Drugs (1890.01.10).

A circa-1900 pill roller on display at Bartell's corporate office in Seattle, December 2009. Courtesy Phil Dougherty.

Another view of Bartell's Denny Building store, 1910s. Courtesy University of Washington Libraries, Special Collections (CFT 0085).

Scales, weights, and medicines from the early twentieth century on display at Bartell's corporate office in Seattle, December 2009. Courtesy Phil Dougherty.

Bartell's peanut brittle on display. Courtesy Bartell Drugs (1930.01.5).

p. 113

A 1920s picture of Bartell and business associates; at least some of the men pictured were managers of his stores. Bartell's long-time associate P.G. Power is behind Bartell and immediately to his right. Courtesy Bartell Drugs (1920.01.4).

George Bartell in the 1920s. Courtesy Bartell Drugs (1918.01.4).

George Bartell Jr. and Beatrice Bartell on a road trip to the mountains, ca. 1924. Courtesy Bartell Drugs (1923.01.2).

Workers in Bartell's photo lab, April 1930. Courtesy Bartell Drugs (1940.01.9).

A Bartell's soda fountain in the 1930s. Courtesy Bartell Drugs.

For many years, Bartell Drugs prepared daily menus for its fountains. Shown is Bartell's University District store fountain menu, November 6, 1926. Courtesy Bartell Drugs.

p. 114

A Bartell photo lab envelope from the late 1930s. Courtesy Bartell Drugs.

1930s streetcar with Bartell Drugs ad. Courtesy Bartell Drugs (1930.01.222).

Bartell's triangle store, 1937. Courtesy Bartell Drugs (1940.01.40).

Bartell's modern Mack Junior delivery truck in action in 1936. Courtesy Bartell Drugs (1930.01.223).

During World War II, Bartell Drugs participated in a drive to collect razors for the men fighting overseas. Courtesy Bartell Drugs (1941.01.1).

A happy crowd rings in New Year's in Seattle and Bartell Drugs is there, 1950s. Courtesy Bartell Drugs (1950.01.35)

p. 115

George D. Bartell, ca. 1961. Courtesy Bartell Drugs (1961.01.10).

Jean Bartell, ca. 1961. Courtesy Bartell Drugs (1961.01.10).

Bartell's Store No. 19 on Roosevelt Way, February 27, 1956. Courtesy Bartell Drugs (1956.01.1).

Bartell's White Center store, ca. 1960. Courtesy Bartell Drugs (1960.01.2).

Bartell's Ballard store in the mid-1960s showing some of the changes brought by self-modernization. Courtesy Bartell Drugs (1960.01.8).

p. 116

Bartell's Magnolia store interior, 1977. Courtesy Bartell Drugs (1977.01.15).

The interior of Bartell's headquarters in 1985 harkened back to an earlier era. Courtesy Bartell Drugs (1985.01.20).

Jean Barber not long after her return to Seattle, August 1991. Courtesy Jean Barber.

George D. Bartell, ca. 1992. Courtesy Bartell Drugs.

The Bartell and Barber families, ca. 1992. Courtesy Bartell Drugs.

Bob and Alina Bartell, 1990s. Courtesy Bartell Drugs.

p. 117

Westlake Park in 2012, on the spot where Bartell's triangle store stood from 1935 until 1984. Courtesy City of Seattle Office of Arts and Culture.

Jean Bartell Barber, ca. 2009. Courtesy Jean Barber.

George Bartell Jr., 1970s. Courtesy Bartell Drugs (1966.01.2).

Bartell and Barber family outing, summer 2010. Courtesy Bartell Drugs.

George D. Bartell and son Mike cutting the ribbon at the grand opening of Bartell's Lake Serene store on July 21, 2009. Courtesy Bartell Drugs.

p. 118

The fourth generation, from left: front: Evelyn Barber and Claire Bartell; rear: Hugh Barber, Mike Bartell, Neal Barber, May 2014. Courtesy Bartell Drugs.

p. 128

Bartell's 1st & Pike store, ca. 1930. Courtesy Bartell Drugs.

Acknowledgements

I want to thank George D. Bartell and Jean Bartell Barber for taking time for several interviews about the history of the Bartell Drug Company and the roles they've both played in that history. Thanks too to Gordon O'Reilly and Val Storrs, who graciously participated in more than a half dozen interviews between them. An appreciative nod likewise goes to Dan Connolly and Peter Koo for their help in providing historical information about pharmacy as well as an overview of pharmacy today and its impact in the twenty-first century.

I'd like to thank Helen Neville, Theron Andrews and Rebecca Siegmund for their assistance in coordinating interviews and research. Kudos too to Mary Ann Klem, Jennifer Kupka, and Sherri Moody for patiently and politely letting me interrupt them in their duties more than once to help walk me through the Bartell archives.

I want to thank two of my colleagues at HistoryLink.org: Tom Brown for his affable editing and writing tips, and Marie McCaffrey for her creative and design tips; it all rounded out the book nicely. A tip of the hat goes to Nancy Kinnear for her design of the book. I'd also like to thank Barry Bartlett for his help in making this all happen. And a grateful thank you goes to Susan and Jenny Dougherty for their support and understanding during this project.

Index

Bartell's
TEA ROOM

Bartells

Bartell

BARTELL DRUGS